PLATO AND CHRISTIAN PERSONALISM

Plato and Christian Personalism

D. T. Sheffler

HILDEBRAND
PROJECT

First Edition 2025 by Hildebrand Press
1235 University Blvd. Steubenville, OH 43952

Copyright © 2025 Dietrich von Hildebrand Legacy Project
All rights reserved

Cataloguing-in-Publication Information
Sheffler, D.T., 1987– | Plato and Christian Personalism / by D.T. Sheffler.— First Edition. Includes bibliographical references, appendix, and index. | Steubenville, OH: Hildbrand Press, 2025.
ISBN 978-1-939773-24-1
Subjects: LCSH: Plato. | Hildebrand, Dietrich von, 1889–1977. | Personalism. | Soul—Philosophy. | Philosophical anthropology. | Self (Philosophy). | BISAC: PHILOSOPHY / History & Surveys / Ancient & Classical | PHILOSOPHY / Metaphysics | PHILOSOPHY / Mind & Body Classification: LCC B398.P47.S54 2025 | DDC 184—dc23

Typeset by Kacbergis Book Design Set in Adobe Caslon

Cover Design by Marylouise McGraw George

Cover Image: J.M.W. Turner, St. Peter's from the South, 1819 Image Source: Public Domain. British Museum, via Wikiart

Front Cover Font: Centaur

Produced by Christopher T. Haley

www.hildebrandproject.org

Contents

Foreword by Mark K. Spencer　xi

Preface　xvii

1. The Personalist Charges against Plato　1
2. Soul, Body, and Person　19
3. Tripartition　63
4. *Nous*, Divinity, and *Theosis*　95
5. Individuality and Uniqueness　129

Index　159

Hildebrand Project

WE ADVANCE THE RICH TRADITION of Christian personalism, especially as developed by Dietrich von Hildebrand and Karol Wojtyla (Pope St. John Paul II), in the service of intellectual and cultural renewal.

Our publications, academic programs, and public events introduce the great personalist thinkers and witnesses of the twentieth century. Animated by a heightened sense of the mystery and dignity of the human person, they developed a personalism that sheds new light on freedom and conscience, the religious transcendence of the person, the relationship between individual and community, the love between man and woman, and the life-giving power of beauty. We connect their vision of the human person with the great traditions of Western and Christian thought, and draw from their personalism in addressing the deepest needs and aspirations of our contemporaries. For more information, please visit: www.hildebrandproject.org

Editorial Board

General Editor: John F. Crosby*
Franciscan University of Steubenville

Rémi Brague
University of Paris, Sorbonne, Emeritus
Romano Guardini Chair of Philosophy,
Ludwig Maximilian University of Munich, Emeritus

Rocco Buttiglione
John Paul II Chair for Philosophy and History of European Institutions
Pontifical Lateran University

Antonio Calcagno
King's University College at The University of Western Ontario

Hanna-Barbara Gerl-Falkovitz
Technische Universität Dresden, Emerita Hochschule Heiligenkreuz

Dana Gioia
Judge Widney Professor of Poetry and Public Culture
University of Southern California

John Haldane
University of St. Andrews
Baylor University

Alice von Hildebrand*†
Widow of Dietrich von Hildebrand

Joseph Koterski, SJ †
Fordham University

Sir Roger Scruton †
Writer and Philosopher

Josef Seifert*
Edith Stein Institute of Philosophy, Granada, Spain

D. C. Schindler
Pontifical John Paul II Institute for Studies on Marriage and Family
Washington, DC

Christoph Cardinal Schönborn
Archbishop Emeritus of Vienna

Fritz Wenisch*†
University of Rhode Island

---

* Student of Dietrich von Hildebrand
† Deceased

Foreword

By Mark K. Spencer

ALFRED NORTH WHITEHEAD famously observed, as D. T. Sheffler reminds us at the end of this book, that the European philosophical tradition can be generally characterized as "a series of footnotes to Plato." But footnotes come in many forms, and for a long time, the footnotes that philosophers have made to Plato, especially in the Christian tradition, have been rather negative. There's something a bit surprising about this. Many of us who have made philosophy our life's work first fell in love with philosophy in large part through reading Plato. Encountering the great Greek philosopher for the first time in causal reading, or in high school or undergraduate introductory courses, has been for many a source of great excitement, from encountering the incomparable character of Socrates, to being initiated into the thrill of serious inquiry, to realizing that one's mind can be raised to transcendent ideas by the sheer force of reasoning.

But if one goes on in philosophy this early fervor about Plato often cools. If one is trained in analytic philosophy, as most aspiring philosophers in the English-speaking world are, then (if one reads more Plato at all) Plato's texts will be reduced to a series of arguments to be analyzed and, for the most part, discarded. The force of Socrates' personality, the shock of insight into the forms, the mystery of the myths with which Plato ends so many of his dialogues will all be ignored. If, instead, one's further education is in Continental philosophy, then often Plato will be presented as the culprit for philosophy's turn away from a direct, living, intense experiential encounter with being itself to a static, ahistorical view of being frozen into concepts and definitions. And if one goes on to study Catholic philosophy, then, as Sheffler explains in chapter 1 of this book, one will likely hear that Plato preaches hatred for the body and that he denies the genuine reality of changing, material particulars, including individual human persons, holding instead that what exists is an unchanging, monistic world of purely abstract ideas. Plato's views, I have often heard it alleged, are completely at odds with the love for persons and for particular material things we find in Christianity, centered as it is on the incarnation, the resurrection, and the sacraments. If one is committed, as both Sheffler and I are, to *personalism*—the school of philosophy that places persons at the center of its metaphysics and its ethics—then Plato might seem like a prime enemy to be avoided, one who is responsible for all the trends in thinking that devalue persons.

The present volume is a welcome and decisive antidote to all these trends. For students and lay readers who have come to love Plato, but who are concerned that his thought is at odds with a commitment to the importance of persons, Sheffler shows that, in fact, Plato's ideas stand behind all the major developments of personalist ideas in Western philosophy. While this book presupposes some familiarity with Plato's dialogues, and while some sections get into technical disputes about textual interpretation, there are many sections of this book, especially in the early chapters, that are easily readable by non-specialists. This book will boost and solidify the excitement over Plato that they naturally feel.

For practicing scholars, Sheffler weighs in on many of the current debates about interpreting Plato, and he shows the systematic coherence and realism of Plato's views. Unlike those scholars who just extract arguments from Plato's texts and analyze them in a modern, rationalistic way, Sheffler is sensitive to the literary qualities of Plato's dialogues as wholes, and to the philosophical importance of the myths, the conversations, and even the deliberately bad arguments found in them. He brings together large-scale analysis of the overall themes of the Platonic corpus with careful textual analysis of particular dialogues, sections, and words to provide a coherent, persuasive view of Platonic philosophy. This is an important work in scholarship on Plato; it could play an important role in reestablishing Platonism as a serious, living, systematic, holistic school of thought in our own times. Indeed, as Sheffler briefly alludes to here, there are ideas about the body, individual uniqueness, liturgy, and divinity in later Platonists like Iamblichus and Proclus that have significant resonances with personalism, and that Christian personalists would also do well to develop.

Of course, as the quotation from Whitehead already shows, scholarship on Plato over the last few centuries has not been as dire as the last few paragraphs make it sound. A small but thriving movement promoting Platonist philosophy as a viable worldview for our times has flourished, and Sheffler draws on some texts from that movement, especially the work of Lloyd Gerson. Over the last half century, some scholars, like Wayne Hankey and Fran O'Rourke, have labored to show how not only the Church Fathers but even Christian thinkers often thought to be anti-Platonic, like Thomas Aquinas, have been deeply indebted to Plato's thought. There have even been lovers of Plato among the personalists. Dietrich von Hildebrand, the personalist to whom Sheffler is most indebted in this volume, makes frequent use of Plato's ideas. Hildebrand defends Plato's emphasis on the importance of the soul over the body. He often adverts to Plato's promotion of the ecstatic experience of "madness" (*mania*) in which one is taken out of oneself by something greater than oneself, as occurs when one is caught up in love. His basic metaphysics is one in which values—ways that things can be important in themselves, such as justice itself or beauty itself—exist in much the same way as Plato's forms, as Hildebrand himself explicitly argues.

The present volume fits beautifully within this context. What Sheffler shows in this book is that, contrary to the criticisms, Plato's ideas stand at the origins of all the core ideas that have come to be central to Christian philosophy in general, and personalist philosophy in particular. He is quite a fair-minded reader of all his source texts, and gives each one its due. He readily grants when a personalist (or other) criticism of Plato is correct—but he also shows how, surprisingly, even those criticisms of Plato are generally rooted in a Platonic insight, which Plato himself just failed to adequately develop. Let me give a brief overview of the highlights of Sheffler's arguments as they unfold over the course of this book.

In chapter 1, after discussing the criticisms levelled against Plato especially by those in the personalist tradition, Sheffler announces his intentions to show that Plato's philosophy is at the origin of a continuous, organic line of development that has flowered into personalism in our own times. Personalism is characterized by a commitment to the idea that "person" is a special category of being, to the central importance of consciousness, self-knowledge, interiority, agency, and freedom, and to the unrepeatable, incommunicable uniqueness and dignity of each person, made in the image of God. While Plato does not explicitly teach or emphasize each of these things, his ideas do undergird each one of them.

In chapter 2, Sheffler shows how Plato's identification of each one of us with our souls, rather than our bodies, is, far from a devaluing of the body, essential for establishing the transcendent importance of persons. Against those who hold that Plato in particular, and the pre-Christian Greeks in general, had no concept of individual persons, Sheffler engages in a careful examination of some of Plato's Greek phrases to show that this is not the case. Even the apparently anti-incarnational idea, found in Plato's *Phaedo*, that the body is the "prison" of the soul comes in for some powerful and persuasive reinterpretation in a personalist direction.

Chapter 3 continues this same line of reasoning, defending Plato's focuses on the centrality of the intellect (*nous*) to persons, on self-knowledge and self-control, and on free self-development. Against those contemporary interpreters who read Plato as holding that our powers—our appetites, our intellect, and so on—are little personlike agents within us, Sheffler shows how Plato is deeply committed to the unity of whole persons. In doing so, Sheffler models how to read Plato platonically. Plato, along with the modern personalists, is committed to the idea that we have a power, the intellect or *nous*, by which we can perceive what things are fundamentally and holistically. Our intellect is not merely a rationalistic power for making logical syllogisms and conceptual distinctions. Sheffler not only helps us see that Plato (and the personalists) saw things this way, but he also educates us, his readers, to see things, especially persons, in this holistic way. In doing so, he also helps us see how working through Plato's texts draws us toward what is highest and best in us, thereby enabling our development *as persons*. I'd suggest that a big part of the excitement we all felt as students in reading Plato—like the excitement Socrates' disciplines had in encountering their master—was that he inspiringly calls us to this development. If you've lost that prospect, this book can return it to you.

That emphasis on what is highest and best in us—that way of reading Plato and the personalists in such a way that doing philosophy becomes, in Pierre Hadot's phrase, a way of life—is continued in chapter 4, which discusses what it is to be divine, for Plato, and the senses in which we human persons are (and can become) divine. A major trend of recent Christian scholarship, in all denominations, has been to recover the idea of deification (*theosis*), which for much of Christian history was seen as the goal of human life, but which has been downplayed by many Christians in recent centuries. Philosophical contemplation (*theoria*), as Plato, Hildebrand, and Sheffler conceive it, is not merely a way of life, but is an initiation into a divine way of life. Just as many contemporary commentators on Plato ignore or downplay his myths, so many reject his talk about the gods. Few have encountered the idea that we should take the idea of the gods seriously, accepting that there really are such beings—and fewer still have retained the idea that these transcendent, but limited, persons are a key part of a Christian vision of life. The idea that reality is populated by many spiritual persons is an idea that personalists above all should accept. This is yet another feature of the tradition that Sheffler's book can restore to those who have lost it.

Finally, in chapter 5, Sheffler argues that, contrary to all the misconceptions, Plato's philosophy is entirely consistent with, and lays the foundations for, a view on which individual persons are unique, unrepeatable, and intrinsically dignified. Here, too, while he engages carefully with scholarly debates, his emphasis is in many ways on the practical effects of doing philosophy platonically. Even when this book doesn't explicitly tell us that that is what it is doing, it is a training in philosophy as a *way of life*. As persons destined for deification, we are called to rise above all that is contingent and merely conventional in us. Much of what we identify as central to our lives in fact consists of mere social identity, attachments to material goods and vices, and temporary feelings and habits. Our uniqueness does not consist in any of those things. Dietrich von Hildebrand seeks those experiences that bid us "lift up our hearts" to what is higher than conventional human life. With St. Paul, we must "seek the things that are above; where Christ is sitting at the right hand of God" (Colossians 3:1). Plato, of course, did not explicitly know Christ. But he too bids us fix our eyes on what is higher, on those truer realities that constitute our actual home. It is in relation to those true realities—those forms and values—that we will fully find our uniqueness and our dignity. Again and again, Sheffler helps us see how Plato's philosophy calls us beyond mere conventionality to authentic human life.

At the end of *The Last Battle*, the final volume of *The Chronicles of Narnia*, by C. S. Lewis, the characters, having died, find themselves in a heavenly country where everything they loved on earth is found again, but in a more real, eternal form. One of the characters, Professor Digory Kirke, explains that our world, the world prior to death, is "only a shadow or copy" of the real world, the world our souls enter into after death. Then he comments that this is "all in Plato." If we listen to Plato's critics, or to his reductionistic interpreters, such a comment sounds quite odd. This book, however, helps us see how right Professor Kirke is: that Plato is the one who first pointed Western thinkers toward the world of true and stable reality, the homeland of the soul, the homeland of human persons. To make one's work a series of footnotes to *that* Plato, as Sheffler has done here, is to live philosophy as it was meant to be lived.

Preface

WE ALL KNOW THE AWKWARD FEELING at parties when two close friends do not seem to get along. Awkwardness turns to tragedy when the distance between the two stems only from mutual misconception. One feels that if they would just meet, just talk for a moment, they would be fast friends before midnight. Such a scenario turns from an ordinary social occurrence to the plot of a novel when the two turn out to be not merely consonant personalities but distant relatives. Such a revelation brings to the foreground all the little details of inherited similarity and even, perhaps, the grounds for their estrangement.

I have long felt that Platonism and Christian personalism are just such a pair, and I have often felt the pain at parties. Personalists, for their part, have often relied heavily on a kind of introductory freshmen exposition of Platonic dualism pitting the soul against the body or universals against particulars, and this misunderstanding has understandably caused them to keep their distance. The Platonists, or at least the contemporary scholars who study Plato, for their part seem blissfully unaware of these aspersions, content to study their period of history and no further.

This book aims to introduce these would-be friends, to pour the wine, and to nudge the conversation toward topics of mutual sympathy. My thesis is that all the central concerns of Christian personalism find their historical origin—though not their full expression and development—in Plato. This is not to say that they are just the same philosophy or agree on every point. Often one philosophy develops some characteristic feature through a strong reaction against a fault in another. Nevertheless, such reactions can take place only against the backdrop of continuity, and even the capacity for reaction relies on a far greater reservoir of shared convictions.

At the very heart of Plato's dialogues lies an intense interest in the self, the true self, the real self, as opposed to all the conventional, social, or distorted self-conceptions that we dream up. This should not surprise anyone who thinks for a moment about the centrality of the Delphic injunction to "know thyself" in several of the dialogues, but the details of many fascinating passages are often missed if one reads Plato only for his theory of the forms or his broader cosmology. One can also miss the breadth of this intense interest across all the dialogues if one focuses attention on a close reading of only one or two—as rewarding as such an exercise can be. Hence, among my chief aims I have tried to simply collect the most important primary texts in one place, present them to the reader side by side, and allow their total mass to establish, little by little, a clear picture of the Platonic philosophy of the self.

This Platonic philosophy of the self involves a spiritualization of the person, insisting that we conceive of ourselves as something more than mere specimens of the mortal human organism, something endowed with mind and therefore bearing the weight of moral agency. In the centuries after Plato, it is just this spiritualization that sets the Platonic school of thought against its Epicurean, Stoic, and to a lesser extent, Aristotelian rivals. Many of the fine points of dispute in the history of metaphysics and epistemology turn precisely on this hinge. As a Christian conception of the person emerges in the following centuries—the conception from which the twentieth-century personalists take their point of departure—the Platonic school contributes far more to its development than the other pagan sources. It is easy to note the points at which Christian anthropology must diverge sharply from pagan Platonism, such as the doctrine of cyclic rebirth, but it is more difficult to appreciate how much the Christian conception depends upon the spiritualization of man that already took place within the Greco-Roman world thanks to Plato and his followers.

This book aims to tell not even a small part of that intervening history but, rather, only the beginning and the end. Of that beginning and end, this book cannot hope to be a comprehensive exposition of either the whole of Plato or the whole of twentieth-century personalism. Instead, I am content simply to gather the chief themes and most relevant primary sources in each. Where these are continuous, I seek to demonstrate this continuity; where there must be a radical break, I seek to identify and explain it.

As contemporary personalism advances the cause of the person, championing our intrinsic worth, dignity, and inner freedom, the Platonic spiritualization of person ought to be a powerful conceptual ally. Furthermore, once this side of Platonism is rightly understood by contemporary personalists, many other unlooked-for allies across the centuries suddenly become more apparent because the influence of Platonism runs so deep and so broad across the whole of Western culture. Hence, I hope that as we pour the wine and encourage a friendly meeting, Christian personalism will come to appreciate just how much his older Platonic cousin has already accomplished and find in those accomplishments the sources of inspiration for further and greater accomplishments of his own.

I want to thank the many conversations and suggestions made to me over several years by my former professors David Bradshaw and Eric Sanday. They are the ones who taught me how to read Plato and oversaw the writing of the dissertation from which this book emerged. I also want to thank those involved with the Hildebrand Project, especially John Henry Crosby, John F. Crosby, Christopher T. Haley, and Mark K.

Spencer for their heroic efforts keeping the flame of personalism alive at their many seminars, symposia, and research initiatives. Many ideas in this book were first drafted during these events. Finally, I am most grateful for the love, support, and honest friendship of my wife, Rose.

D. T. Sheffler

PLATO AND CHRISTIAN PERSONALISM

CHAPTER I

The Personalist Charges against Plato

TO THE CASUAL OBSERVER, the emergence of personalist philosophy in the twentieth century may appear to be a quintessentially modern phenomenon. Such an observer might be forgiven for thinking that personalism principally comes from critical turning points in post-Enlightenment thinking that represent a radical rupture with everything that came before. Perhaps the personalist concern for interiority comes from the "inward turn" that happens in European thinking following Descartes. Perhaps the insistence that human persons are to be treated with dignity comes from Kantian ethics. Perhaps the emphasis on talk about the self and one's agency comes from existentialism or a Nietzschean self-assertive will to power. Although suggestive, these possibilities retain their plausibility only so long as our observer remains ignorant of premodern philosophy and theology. There are developments, of course, but only someone who has never read the medieval mystics could think there was no concern for interiority before Descartes. Only someone unfamiliar with the philosophy of Plotinus or the Stoics could think that an emphasis on the self is exclusively modern.

To a less casual observer, the emergence of personalist philosophy may appear to be an especially Thomistic movement. Thomistic revivalists such as Étienne Gilson and Jacques Maritain certainly hold a prominent place among personalist thinkers, and *they*, at any rate, insist upon the centrality of St. Thomas in their account of the history. A curious feature of these Thomistic personalists, however, is that they tend to see St. Thomas's philosophy in particular and Christian philosophy more generally as a radical break from Platonic philosophy, especially when it comes to their account of the person. This is all the more curious since St. Thomas himself draws so heavily on the Platonic tradition of St. Augustine, the *Corpus Dionysticum*, and the *Liber De Causis*. Might there not be more alliance than opposition between Thomistic personalism and the Platonic tradition, especially with regard to the person?

Some might find it awkward that a thoroughly pagan thinker should loom so large in the history of such a Christian idea, but I am inclined to see this very continuity between pagan and Christian thought as a vindication of universal truth. We should ask ourselves why nearly all the early Christian authors find so much congenial to their faith in Platonism. Indeed, this very congeniality motivated them to devote special attention to those places where the Platonic and Christian account of the person are actually at odds. Family squabbles are often the most intense. Such disputes draw the energy for their particular conflicts from the enormous reservoir of shared sentiment.

This book attempts to set the record straight by carefully examining the most relevant passages from Plato's dialogues and demonstrating the continuity, where it exists, between these texts and contemporary personalism. Conversely, this must require an honest look at those places where personalist thought requires either extensive development and revision of Plato's ideas or an outright rejection. In order to make this more nuanced examination of the relationship between Plato and personalism, I will draw on several authors who exemplify the personalist movement, but I will take Dietrich von Hildebrand's phenomenology as an especially valuable model for several reasons. First, Hildebrand's realist metaphysics and concern for the spiritual dimension displays a profound sympathy with the basic Platonic project. Second, Hildebrand elaborates his personalism from a phenomenological basis free from some of the historical theses that we will see cloud the judgment of Gilson and those who follow him vis-a-vis Plato. Third, Hildebrand's account of the human person is multifaceted enough that it will provide numerous opportunities to find both continuity with and dissent from Platonic ideas.

This more nuanced approach is, I hope, an improvement on the comments concerning Plato from personalist authors that I will examine in detail in the next section. In each of the following cases, personalist authors have done Plato a disservice by characterizing his view of the person in broad brush strokes without examining any actual texts. Once his actual writing is put side by side with the claims made about him, we will be in a much better position to judge just how much contemporary personalist thought owes to Plato.

What Is Supposed to be Missing from Plato?

We can begin by examining the accounts given by four influential twentieth-century personalists who all agree that the Platonic worldview has no room for the concept of person, although they differ on the details. I want to examine these details because the specific charges brought against Plato will provide a number of anchor points as we examine the Platonic material in later chapters.

To my knowledge, the earliest version of the personalist case against Plato can be found in Étienne Gilson's widely read *Spirit of Mediaeval Philosophy*:

> In a doctrine like Plato's it is not at all this Socrates, however highly extolled he may be, that matters: it is Man. If Socrates has any importance at all it is only because he is an exceptionally happy, but at the same time quite accidental, participation in the being of an Idea. The idea of Man is eternal, immutable, necessary; Socrates, like all other individuals, is only a temporary and accidental being; he partakes of the unreality of his matter, in which the permanence of the idea is reflected, and his merely momentary being flows away on the stream of becoming. Certain

individuals, no doubt, are better than others, but that is not in virtue of any unique character, bound up with and altogether inseparable from their personality, it is simply because they participate more or less fully in a common reality, that is to say this ideal type of humanity which, being one and the same for all men, is alone truly real.[1]

Gilson makes this claim at the beginning of his chapter entitled "Christian Personalism," and he goes on to give an account of the development of the concept of the person in Christian thought against the backdrop of this ostensible failure in Plato's metaphysics (along with a slightly different failure in Aristotle's). But is it really credible to think that the author of the *Symposium* fails to give any importance to the individuality of Socrates? Is it really credible to think that a whole corpus of dialogues systematically devoting so much attention to the care of the soul and the Delphic injunction to "know thyself" treats the individual person as a "merely momentary being" that "flows away on the stream of becoming"?

Gilson seems to think that the metaphysical status of the person *Socrates* appears in the dialogues uniformly as a concrete particular to be treated just like any other concrete particular in contrast to the eternal forms. This is perhaps because Gilson thinks that the name *Socrates* refers to the composite of soul and body that, for Plato, must pass away at death. Several texts that we will examine, however, suggest that *Socrates* does not fit neatly into a simple form–particular dichotomy because the person is consistently identified in the dialogues with the soul rather than the soul–body composite. We will also see that the soul for Plato occupies a middle ground, acting as a kind of bridge *between* the worlds of Being and Becoming. This identification of the person with the soul leads to several problems that we will explore in later chapters, but it does not lead to the problem that Gilson describes.

Our second author, Joseph Ratzinger, in his influential essay "Concerning the Notion of Person in Theology," takes this line of thinking

---

[1]. Étienne Gilson, *The Spirit of Mediaeval Philosophy* (Notre Dame, IN: University of Notre Dame Press, 1936), 190–91.

further, acknowledging his dependence on Gilson explicitly. According to Ratzinger, the concept of person is wholly the product of Christian theology, emerging out of early Christian disputes about the person of Christ. In the Trinitarian theology of Nicea, Christ is one person, distinct from the Father, yet "consubstantial" with him. In the theology of the incarnation after Chalcedon, Christ is one person in two natures, fully God and fully man. Clearly, the concept of "person" is doing a lot of theological work in both these doctrinal formulations.

The historical details here are a little messier than Ratzinger lets on, however. The Greek term ὑπόστασις is not used at Nicea in its later technical sense—indeed those who say that the Son is a distinct hypostasis from the Father are anathematized—and even once the term is more clearly defined in the late fourth century it does not so closely match the concept of "person" as the Latin translation into *persona* suggests (and the Greek term πρόσωπον is not always an equivalent). The messiness here need not detain us, however. What matters for our purposes is Ratzinger's central claim: "The concept of the person is thus, to speak with Gilson, one of the contributions to human thought made possible and provided by Christian faith." The concept, Ratzinger contends, is wholly absent in pre-Christian Greek thinking. It was only when "faith began to reflect" that "Christian thought made use of the philosophically insignificant or entirely unused concept" of person.[2]

According to Ratzinger, this early Trinitarian and Christological reflection comes to fruition only centuries later in the definition of person by Richard of St. Victor as *spiritualis naturae incommunicabilis existentia*. This definition locates the "theological meaning" of the concept of person on the level of existence rather than essence. Pre-Christian philosophy failed to see this, Ratzinger says, because "in Antiquity philosophy was limited entirely to the level of essence."[3] From the side of Trinitarian theology, if Christians affirm that God is three Persons and one substance, then the conception of divine Person in play cannot be collapsed

---

2. Joseph Ratzinger, "Concerning the Notion of Person in Theology," trans. Michael Waldstein, *Communio* 17, no. 3 (1990): 439–40.

3. Ibid., 449.

to a particular kind of substance without contradiction. From the side of Christology, if Christians affirm that Christ is one person who possesses two complete natures, then the conception of person in play cannot be collapsed to one or the other nature or even any part of either nature without contradiction.

Granting that Plato does not have exactly the later Latin distinction between *essentia* and *existentia* (although he does use τὸ εἶναι and οὐσία in slightly different ways), it seems a stretch to say that Plato entirely ignores the existential dimension of personal reality. Following Gilson, Ratzinger seems to conceive of Plato's metaphysics (and Greek metaphysics generally) as an entirely two-level system comprising universal essences and the "merely momentary being" of concrete particulars, that is, Being and Becoming. But again, this ignores the mediating place of soul in Plato's metaphysics, not to mention all those, such as Aristotle and the Stoics, who are inspired by him to one degree or another in this respect. Also granting that the pre-Christians do not have precisely the categories that Christians needed to articulate Trinitarian and Christological theology—after all, why would they?—for long centuries these theologically precise notions play almost no role in Christian philosophical anthropology. When Christians do engage in attempts to define the *human* person, the result is just as likely to be influenced by the Platonic tradition of spirituality, in which the noetic soul reascends to its source through contemplation, as it is likely to be influenced by specifically Christian doctrines, such as the resurrection of the body or the incarnation of Christ.

In several ways the criticisms of Karol Wojtyła, in his essay "Subjectivity and the Irreducible in the Human Being," are different from the other authors we are considering in this section. In the first place, he does not name Plato or speak about Greek philosophy in general. Instead, he identifies the "traditional Aristotelian anthropology" that defines man in terms of genus and deferentia: ὁ ἄνθρωπος νοητικόν. In the second place, he focuses on the newness that we find in a contemporary, phenomenological approach to philosophy rather than the newness that we find in early Christianity. Nevertheless, I want to include this short but loaded essay in our discussion here because it puts a finger on several personalist concerns that are frequently thought to be absent in Greek philosophy.

Wojtyła calls the "traditional Aristotelian anthropology" the "cosmological" understanding of the human person that would affirm the "reducibility of the human being to the world."[4] Wojtyła claims that this is a constant danger in the Aristotelian tradition because definitions of the kind we see in Aristotle and Boethius have the tendency to treat the human person as "mainly an object, something that is merely one of the objects in the world to which the human being visibly and physically belongs."[5] This way of understanding the human person, however, leaves out "the revelation of the person as a subject *experiencing* its acts and inner happenings, and with them its own subjectivity."[6] Hence we must introduce "the aspect of *consciousness*" into the analysis of the human person. In consequence of introducing this element of subjectivity that cannot be reduced to a purely objective analysis of the world, we will appreciate "that which is unique and unrepeatable in each human being, by virtue of which he or she is not just *a particular human being*—an individual of a certain species—but *a personal subject*."[7] At the same time, Wojtyła is concerned to make sure we understand that "the personalistic type of understanding the human being is not the antinomy of the cosmological type but its complement."[8] This is so because the human being, besides being an unrepeatable subject, really is a determinate object in the world belonging to a certain species. We can understand this subjectivity *within* "the *objective totality* that goes by the name *human being*."[9]

As we will see in much more detail in the following chapters, I believe that Plato does open a door to this kind of thinking, while perhaps doing less than we might desire in the way of explicit argumentation and

---

4. Karol Wojtyła, "Subjectivity and the Irreducible in the Human Being," in *Person and Community: Selected Essays*, ed. Theresa Sandok (New York: Peter Lang, 1993), 211.
5. Ibid.
6. Ibid., 213 (emphasis in original).
7. Ibid., 214 (emphasis in original).
8. Ibid., 213.
9. Ibid., 216 (emphasis in original).

analysis. Plato certainly devotes a great deal of space in his dialogues to thinking about what it means to be a knower, and this involves an analysis of what may justly be called "consciousness," especially consciousness of the forms. Again, we must expand the typical two-category account of Plato to a three-category account. In addition to form and participant, we must add mind (νοῦς), a subject about which he is by no means silent. Furthermore, we will see that many passages in the dialogues identify the true or ideal self with the noetic part of the soul as it is capable of becoming conscious of the forms. A promising start to a more "personalistic type of understanding." While this may well escape the danger of thinking of ourselves as merely "one of the objects in the world to which the human being visibly and physically belongs," it may simply replace thinking of the person as a specimen of a biological species with thinking of the person as a specimen of a psychic or noetic species. Furthermore, we will see that the contents of what each perfectly noetic soul thinks ultimately converges on a qualitatively identical object. There may be as many numerically distinct centers of consciousness as there are souls, but any qualitative divergence in what these souls think must be a departure from the perfect activity of νοῦς. Granting, therefore, that an analysis of consciousness does not lead Plato to an analysis of "that which is unique and unrepeatable in each human being," this is a more nuanced critique than the charge that Plato simply has no appreciation for subjectivity, interiority, or consciousness.

More recently from the Eastern Orthodox perspective, Metropolitan John D. Zizioulas has advanced similar claims in the first chapter of his *Being and Communion*. The first section, "From Mask to Person: The Birth of an Ontology of Personhood," presents Zizioulas's version of the historical thesis that "[t]he person both as a concept and as a living reality is purely the product of patristic theology and ecclesiology."[10] Zizioulas begins this section with a claim that sounds very much like Gilson's above. In Platonic philosophy, he says, "[e]verything concrete and 'individual' is ultimately referred to the abstract idea which constitutes

---

10. John Zizioulas, *Being as Communion* (Crestwood, NY: St. Vladimir's Seminary Press, 1997), 27.

its ground and final justification."[11] For Zizioulas, it is important that we conceive of the person as unique, unrepeatable, free, and fully real. Platonism, for Zizioulas, is just one expression of the deep monistic trend in all Greek thinking that traces all difference and multiplicity back to "the 'one' being." Hence, the uniqueness and unrepeatability of the person must signal a "'fall' from being."[12] Zizioulas's second observation about Platonism, however, goes deeper:

> In Platonic thought the person is a concept which is ontologically impossible, because the soul, which ensures man's continuity, is not united permanently with the concrete, "individual" man: it lives eternally but it can be united with another concrete body and can constitute another "individuality," e.g. by reincarnation.[13]

Zizioulas interprets *Timaeus* 41d–e as saying that all souls are qualitatively identical until they enter into bodies and it is only through embodiment that anything like a distinct personality could arise.[14] On this reading, then, Plato's ontology of the human being fails to make possible the concept of person because it locates that which is most real and endures, on the one hand, with the soul and locates the concrete individual personality, on the other hand, with the composite of soul and body. In a footnote, Zizioulas acknowledges the possibility that the soul itself could take on differentiating features as a result of its embodiment, a possibility to which we will have occasion to return, but he thinks that successive reincarnations, even into animal bodies, precludes the single soul that animates these various lives from developing "a distinct 'personality' of its own on the basis of a particular body."[15]

Our next author, C. J. De Vogel, differs from the others by dissenting

---

11. Ibid., 27–28.
12. Ibid., 29.
13. Ibid., 28.
14. The key sentence of the *Timaeus* passage that Zizioulas seems to have in mind is: "They [the lesser souls] would all be assigned one and the same initial birth, so that none would be less well treated by him [the Demiurge] than any other" (*Timaeus* 41e, trans. Donald J. Zeyl). Unless otherwise indicated, all Plato quotations are from Plato, *Complete Works*, ed. John M. Cooper (Indianapolis: Hackett Publishing Company, 1997).
15. Zizioulas, *Being as Communion*, 28 n. 2.

from Gilson and the general consensus we see in those who follow him. She argues that the pagan Greeks did indeed possess the concept of person, and she finds that "the first metaphysics of man as a moral person is found in Greek philosophy, and of man in his individuality as well."[16] She begins by helpfully drawing a distinction between the notion of *person* and the notion of *personality*. The former she defines as "man as a rational being and moral subject, free and self-determining in his actions, responsible for his deeds." The latter she defines as "man's individual character, his uniqueness."[17] With respect to a philosophy of the *person*, De Vogel finds ample reflection on moral agency and responsibility beginning as early as the Pythagoreans and Heraclitus, but cropping up again and again as an important concern in all the major philosophical schools. She mentions that at least since Locke, the criterion of self-consciousness or self-reflection on one's agency is added as an essential element of the concept of *person*. She shows that this element, while perhaps less prevalent in ancient theories, is nevertheless present, especially in the Stoics and Plotinus.[18] With respect to the concept of *personality*, De Vogel cites several examples from Greek literature that bring the unique personality of heroic characters to the forefront, such as Achilles, Antigone, or Socrates. She does, however, concede that the Greeks "were not interested in [individuality] *in the same way* as moderns often are," as evidenced by the fact that they "never produced such a *genre* as modern psychological novel."[19]

I have discussed De Vogel at length only because she is responding directly to Gilson's argument. A similar approach, however, is found more recently by several other scholars. Christopher Gill finds many, many places throughout Greek philosophy, epic, and drama that emphasize the uniqueness, self-awareness, and vibrant personality of individuals.[20]

---

16. C. J. De Vogel, "The Concept of Personality in Greek and Christian Thought," in *Studies in Philosophy and the History of Philosophy*, ed. Ryan John Kenneth (Washington, DC: The Catholic University of America Press, 1963), 22.
17. Ibid., 23.
18. Ibid., 24.
19. Ibid., 29.
20. Christopher Gill, "Is There a Concept of the Person in Greek Philosophy," in *Psychology*, ed. Stephen Everson (Cambridge: Cambridge University Press, 1991), 166–93; *Personality in Greek Epic, Tragedy, and Philosophy* (Oxford: Oxford University Press, 1996).

Richard Sorabji likewise argues that Greek authors do display in various ways a conception of the person or the self.[21] Anthony Long describes the models of self-consciousness that are central to Greek philosophical systems, Plato not least among them, and the spiritualities that follow them.[22] Although he does not discuss the concept of person specifically, Michael Frede makes a similar argument regarding free will, locating its origin among the Stoics.[23]

What Is Personalism?

Unfortunately, the nature of the term "person" exacerbates the confusion of this debate considerably. Because the word "person" is common in everyday speech, it covers a wide semantic range that remains fuzzy at the edges. Because the word also denotes a central concept in many philosophical systems and Trinitarian theology, all the authors involved in the debate employ their own very precise usage. As a result, those who side with Gilson say, "Here is concept covered by the term 'person,' and the Greeks do not have it," while those who dissent along with De Vogel say, "Here is concept covered by the term 'person,' and the Greeks do have it." Both and are within the semantic range of the English word "person," and both authors are largely correct in their analysis of the Greek material, but an apparent controversy has been created.

On the one hand, those who side with Gilson frequently adopt a very stringent view of what it means to have a concept of person. Although they differ in the details, Wojtyła, Ratzinger, and Zizioulas all have a sophisticated and precise account of the way that the Christian concept of person is irreducible to the category of nature. On the other hand, those who dissent along with De Vogel frequently seem to adopt more broad and easily satisfied criteria for a culture's displaying an awareness of the concept. On this approach, a text succeeds in displaying the concept of

---

21. Richard Sorabji, *Self* (Chicago: The University of Chicago Press, 2006).
22. A. A. Long, *Greek Models of Mind and Self* (Cambridge, MA: Harvard University Press, 2015).
23. *A Free Will*, ed. A. A. Long (Berkeley: University of California Press, 2012).

person if it describes the kinds of behaviors or qualities we take persons to exemplify, such as moral responsibility, rationality, or the individual flare of distinctive personalities. Given that the pagan authors were thoughtful human beings living among other human beings, I find it hard to see how they *could* fail to reflect at least sometimes on such subjects. We would have to think Gilson, Wojtyła, Ratzinger, and Zizioulas to be very ignorant indeed if we understood them to be making such an argument. If by "concept of person" we simply mean "concept of moral responsibility" or "concept of an individual human being," then the Greeks in general and Plato in particular doubtless possess such a concept, and it will not be difficult to find particular texts that demonstrate this awareness.

I propose, therefore, to shift the terms of this debate. Rather than asking whether Plato possesses a "concept of person," we should ask whether we can find continuity or discontinuity with *personalism*. To be fair, this is actually how Gilson originally put the question, but the conversation has drifted. Furthermore, I propose that we should not treat personalism as a singular thesis that can be evaluated simply as present or absent from a text. Rather, we should treat personalism as an attitude toward the value of the person, a concern for thinking about the person as a person. From this attitude a whole nexus of concerns arise. Historically, twentieth-century personalism as a philosophical movement arises out of several such concerns, each of which has a complex historical development. Once we tease these historical threads of development apart, we will see that Gilson is partly vindicated and partly refuted. Some of these threads are central to the thought of Plato and may very well go back before him to Pythagorean, Orphic, or Eleatic sources. On these themes, Plato should be read as a proto-personalist, an important source for many of the more developed philosophies and spiritualities that follow. Some threads, however, are either entirely absent or at least very thinly present in Plato, and the twentieth-century personalists are right to emphasize their departure from him.

I propose eleven such threads that braid together to make the historical cord of personalism:

Persons as a Special Category—Sometimes this idea revolves around human beings as a species set apart from all other species. Sometimes, however, angels or deities are also included in the special category.[24] Classically, the distinguishing feature of the category is typically rationality, construed in one way or another, but it may also be immortality of soul, moral responsibility, or freedom of will. It is hard to see how any philosophy could fail to distinguish human beings in some way from other animals. What matters for personalism is the recognition that human beings are special in some way *as persons*, as someones rather than merely somethings alongside other somethings in the cosmos.

Consciousness—Persons appear not simply as objects in the world but also as knowing subjects. Hildebrand describes the way that the Greeks, as opposed to the earlier Assyrians and Phoenicians, developed a sense of "distance" between man and the world, looking upon it with wonder.[25] The question of knowledge and all its attendant problems is, of course, classical, but what the personalist emphasizes is a sensitivity to the distinctive dimension that being a knowing, conscious subject involves. We will see that far from being absent, this theme is front and center in the dialogues.

Self-Knowledge—The Delphic injunction to "know thyself" and Socrates' unique interpretation of it begins a whole tradition in Western thought around the importance of self-knowledge. In the Platonic material, as we will see, this usually takes the form of perplexity about the kind of being that one is rather than a quest to know one's self as an individual. Nevertheless, this encourages a kind of introspection that readily produces the latter preoccupation, as it does, for example, in St. Augustine.[26]

Interiority—Once we begin that inward turn in the history of philosophy, the inner dimension of the soul begins to open up for our exploration. Philip Cary argues that this experience of a whole world within begins with St. Augustine, but we will see that there is at least some

---

24. Dietrich von Hildebrand, *Ethics* (Steubenville, OH: Hildebrand Press, 2020), 180.
25. Dietrich von Hildebrand, *Graven Images* (Steubenville, OH: Hildebrand Press, 2019), 27.
26. See the entire chapter devoted to self-knowledge in Dietrich von Hildebrand, *Transformation in Christ* (Manchester, NH: Sophia Institute Press, 1990).

precedent in Plato, not to mention other sources such as the Stoics or the authors of the Psalms.²⁷

The True Self—The Delphic injunction also raises the important question—repeatedly in the Platonic dialogues—whether various candidates for the self are really the *true* self. I may think, for example, that the pose I put on for others or my social rôle is really me, but upon reflection I discover that it is far from being the true me at all. Importantly for the whole Platonic tradition Socrates asks whether the body or the soul–body composite is the true self. Even within the soul, we may ask whether various psychic subcomponents are the true self. The experience, therefore, of finding alien aspects even of one's own psychology is hardly a discovery of modern depth psychology. This thread, however, leads to one of the most important points of disagreement between personalism and the Platonic tradition. In the dialogues, we see an ever more narrow identification of the true self, first with the soul then with the noetic aspect of the soul. Even here, thinkers in the Platonic tradition go further, identifying a really true self even within the mind, the highest summit of the noetic soul that touches upon Νοῦς itself. This consistent push to identify with a more and more narrow element within the human totality and therefore alienate everything else, has a multitude of important ramifications both in philosophical theory and in spiritual practice. Personalists, by contrast, have insisted on identifying the human self with the whole human being and have refused to alienate our bodies or the "lower" aspects of our psychology such as our affectivity.²⁸

Agency and Freedom—A related but distinct thread all the way through the history concerns thinking about agency and passivity. A person, it is thought, is understood as the author of his own actions, responsible for them and endorsing them in some way. The arrow fired by the archer, by contrast, stands in a wholly passive relation to its own motion. Once we recognize this distinction, however, we become aware that many things that go on within ourselves are passive and not subject to our agency, at least not immediately. We may rightly ask, then, what the ultimate

---

27. Phillip Cary, *Augustine's Invention of the Inner Self* (Oxford: Oxford University Press, 2000).
28. Juan Manuel Burgos, *Personalist Anthropology* (Wilmington, DE: Vernon Press, 2022), 4.

source of our actions is and what it takes to be considered the genuine author of them. From this comes a deep concern for the whole nexus of questions connected to fate, providence, and freedom. According to Hildebrand, persons are revealed as persons most of all in their free response to objective value. This freedom is an actualization of what he terms our "free spiritual center," from which we give our ultimate "yes" or "no."[29] Far from a purely modern conception, this idea has clear antecedents in the Stoic notion of the ἡγεμονικόν. Philosophically we find many of these ideas at least as early as the Myth of Er in the *Republic*, but this theme is also, of course, a central preoccupation of even earlier Greek tragedy.

Personal Identity—The question of personal identity is really two questions: (i) What makes a person the same person across time? (ii) What makes one person distinct from other persons? We can find some curiosity about such questions in the ancient sources, but they tend to be the general metaphysical questions of qualitative and numerical identity, and the answers that ancient philosophers give apply just as well to particular horses or particular pebbles. Contemporary philosophers, however, have become more and more interested in asking these questions specifically of persons since the answers we give have immediate relevance for the questions of agency, the true self, punishment and reward, and survival after death. There is, indeed, *some* reflection on specifically personal identity, but it may appear to be more than it actually is because of the habit, since Aristotle, of using Socrates as a stock logical example (or Dion and Theon among the Stoics) when discussing the puzzles surrounding the metaphysics of identity in general.

Uniqueness of Individuals—This is tied in with the last theme because one solution to the question of identity is to posit some feature of individual persons that is necessarily unique, whether that be a particular chunk of matter, an individuating form, or a unique bundle of attributes. What matters in this distinct thread, however, is not simply accounting for personal identity but the conviction that each and every person is *special* in some way, that each is an unrepeatable being without which the universe would suffer a loss. This may come from an intuition about

---

29. Hildebrand, *Ethics*, 309; *Transformation in Christ*, 62–67.

the specialness of particular outstanding persons, such as Socrates or a beloved friend, but it may also take the form of a general intuition about all persons as persons. Both De Vogel and Gill argue that the ancients are aware in their literature of the specialness of unique outstanding individuals such as Achilles or Aeneas, but there is some gap historically between characterizing this uniqueness in literary portrayals and accounting for it philosophically. Juan Burgos argues that such philosophical awareness follows only the deep ethical revolution occasioned by the Christian insistence that in Christ there is no longer any discrimination between Jew or Greek, slave or free, male or female.[30]

Incommunicability—In jurisprudence, there has been some reflection on these questions because the Roman legal conception of *persona* determines who holds property and who possesses rights, some of which are *communicabiles* (that is, transferable) while some are *incommunicabiles* (that is, nontransferable). The Roman legal definition of a person is: *Persona est sui iuris et alteri incommunicabilis*.[31] This legal terminology provides the vocabulary that makes possible Ratzinger's preferred definition of person, coming from Richard of St. Victor in the twelfth century: *spiritualis naturae incommunicabilis existentia* (an incommunicable existence of a spiritual nature). This ultimately leads to a whole range of considerations that revolve around the notion that there is some core of the person that is entirely his own, which cannot be shared with another or replicated even in principle.[32] It is sometimes thought that Plato's conception of the noetic soul is incompatible with this incommunicability because each mind is thought ultimately to merge with every other.[33] As we will explore later, however, this is far from clear in the text of the dialogues, and Lloyd Gerson has argued that a plurality of minds that are necessarily numerically distinct is entirely consistent with what the dialogues do say.[34]

---

30. Burgos, *Personalist Anthropology*, 17.

31. John Crosby, *The Selfhood of the Human Person* (Washington, DC: The Catholic University of America Press, 1996), 7.

32. See further the excellent chapter "Incommunicability" in ibid.

33. Julia Annas, "Self Knowledge in Early Plato," in *Platonic Investigations*, ed. Dominic J. O'Meara (Washington, DC: The Catholic University of America Press, 1985), 130–31; G. M. A. Grube, *Plato's Thought* (Boston: Beacon Press, 1964), 148.

34. Lloyd Gerson, *Knowing Persons* (Oxford: Oxford University Press, 2003), 193.

Imago Dei—A central tenet of Christian teaching on the human person is that man is made in the image of God. This means not only that human beings are distinct from all the other animal species on Earth, but also that there is something divine about us. This link between man and God grounds the whole quest of the spiritual life. Man must elevate and prioritize what is divine over that which is earthly, and he must seek to reunite with his Creator by participating in his nature (*theosis*). Although he is not drawing from Genesis (*pace* Justin Martyr), we certainly find in Plato the idea that human beings have a divine core and that this provides the basis for the spiritual quest. Little wonder that very early on Christians were especially drawn to this aspect of the Platonic tradition. Despite this congeniality, there is also a gulf, as Hildebrand argues, between pantheistic or polytheistic conceptions of divinity and the conception of a God who is at once fully personal and infinite, a gulf that has a profound influence on how one conceives of the metaphysical status of man as image of God standing before God.[35]

Dignity—All of the above point to a notion that is sometimes thought to originate with Kant: the idea that persons, just by being persons, possess universal and intrinsic moral worth. A whole range of political and ethical ideas issue from this, from the Kantian insistence that persons are never to be used merely as a means to the foundation for universal political rights. As John Crosby so poignantly argues, *something must be absent* from the ancient understanding of the person given the way that all ancient philosophers seem entirely blind to the intrinsic violation of dignity involved in the institution of slavery.[36] Nevertheless, their own theories do provide some basis for the recognition of intrinsic dignity, whether they saw their way to this conclusion or not. In Plato's case, we find the idea that every human being must be ensouled, not with just any soul, but with a soul capable of apprehending the forms, and this betrays their divine origin.

---

35. Hildebrand, *Transformation in Christ*, 163–66.
36. Crosby, *The Selfhood of the Human Person*, 13.

One final note about the discussion of continuity and development of these ideas: When we look for the historical development of ideas within a tradition, we must look for more than mere similarity. We might notice points of similarity or contrast, for example, between Plato's conception of cosmic Νοῦς and the Vedic conception of *dharma*. Nevertheless, it would be a historical mistake to read either as a development of the other. But we must also not insist upon exact citation or perfect terminological consistency. For example, the Myth of Er does not quite say everything we might think it says about free will. Indeed, the language of "free will" does not appear in the text, and we should rightly advise caution about reading later ideas anachronistically into the *Republic*. Nevertheless, it is easy to see how the Myth of Er might suggest questions of freedom and fate, responsibility and predestination, to later authors who *do* use and develop the notion of free will. Hence, we might see these later authors as carrying forward a philosophical conversation in continuity with Plato even though they extend its range considerably.

We must also warn against a certain set of important difficulties peculiar to the interpretation of Plato. Since Plato wrote only dialogues (and perhaps a letter or two) we rarely if ever find anything that we can attribute straightforwardly to him. He puts ideas forward in the mouth of many characters, most notably Socrates, and just because he represents Socrates as uttering certain ideas, we cannot infer directly that this is Plato's position. Indeed, it may not even be Socrates' position since there is a large gap between the historical Socrates and the Socrates represented in the dialogues, and even here, Socrates is known for his irony. Fortunately, for our purposes most of these difficulties are moot. We are interested in the historical development of personalist ideas, and for this project it is largely irrelevant what Plato truly believed in his heart of hearts. It also matters little whether certain dialogues are genuine or not or whether critical passages are in the mode of myth or dialectic. These things matter greatly for the accurate interpretation of Plato, and we will do our best to be sensitive to these issues, but for the historical project, what really matters is that certain ideas appear at a certain date in the classical world attached to the name of Plato.

CHAPTER 2

Soul, Body, and Person

IN ORDER TO SLAY THE BIGGEST CYCLOPS FIRST, we begin our examination at the point of greatest tension between Platonism and personalism, the ostensible alienation of the body from the true self. "Everybody knows" that Plato advocates a radical dualism and that this has historically led to a whole anti-body cast of mind with numerous ramifications in philosophy, spirituality, and even ordinary ways of speaking about ourselves. Contemporary thinkers generally, and personalists especially, view this anti-body cast of mind with horror, and this has led to two opposite and equally erroneous ways of reading Plato. First, those without any special fondness for Plato take the dualism as grounds for reading Plato as an opponent of personalism and thereby miss the deep affinity with personalism on other points. Second, those who have fallen in love with one or another aspect of Plato take their admiration on these other points as grounds for thinking that Plato could not really have meant what they find so horrifying about dualism.

Admittedly, there *are* a few textual reasons for thinking that the anti-body attitude may not be as thoroughgoing as it first appears from a first reading of the *Phaedo*. First, steps in the logic of many other dialogues suggest a more favorable attitude toward the body than that presented in the *Phaedo*. For example, bodily *eros* is the first rung in the *Symposium*'s Ladder of Love, the good governance of the cosmos requires that soul looks after body in the *Timaeus* and the *Phaedrus*, and a positive role is given to bodily pleasure in the *Philebus*. Second, many of the relevant passages are couched in myth, which Socrates and other characters flag numerous times as standing in contrast to more literal and serious dialectic. This might raise some doubts about how exactly we are to take the stories of souls being reincarnated as bees. Third, the logic of many of the dialectical arguments themselves, especially those in the *Phaedo*, are notoriously fallacious in ways that the characters in the dialogues immediately interrogate. Obviously, the ironic and provoking Socrates cannot always be taken at face value.[1]

Nevertheless, a personalist reading of the material cannot ignore or minimize the anti-body picture that does clearly emerge not only from the *Phaedo* but across several texts. Not all the relevant material is in the form of myth. Much of it, in the *Alcibiades*, *Phaedo*, *Phaedrus*, and *Laws*, takes the form of strongly worded dialectical argument. When it does come to the many myths, although we cannot take them literally or stitch their divergent details into a single Platonic cosmology, we *can* come away with a surprisingly consistent general picture of our postmortem fate. Taken with a dash of allegory, the myths can be made to yield a compellingly comprehensive picture of death and rebirth. This feature of the myths gains historical influence through those many readers who have taken belief in an afterlife seriously and have sought answers from Plato. This picture differs dramatically from that required by its historical alternatives: on the one hand a commitment to personal mortality by the Peripatetics, Stoics, and Epicureans and, on the other, a commitment to immortality without cyclic rebirth by the Christians.

---

1. See, for example, Ronna Burger, *The Phaedo: A Platonic Labyrinth* (New Haven, CT: Yale University Press, 1984), who pushes this logic so far as to make Socrates in the *Phaedo* say almost the exact opposite of his apparent meaning.

The Platonic Model

We can summarize the general picture briefly as follows. With consistent terminology, Plato distinguishes explicitly between three things that are treated as discrete substances:

1. The body (σῶμα)
2. The soul (ψυχή)
3. The compound of the two, a temporary mortal organism (ζῷον)

A single immortal soul cyclically enters into a compound of a certain structure (φύσις, εἶδος, σχῆμα) to form a single mortal organism. While it is a member of this compound structure, the soul lives a temporary life (βίος) that runs from the birth of the compound (γένεσις) to its death (θάνατος). In our own case, we happen to find ourselves embodied in a particular form of mortal organic life, which he calls the "human being" (ἄνθρωπος). The kind of compound that the soul can enter into is shaped by the past that it has lived so far—determined partially by divine allotment (κλήρωσις) and partially by its own choice (αἵρεσις). Because the structure of the human organism (ἀνθρώπου εἶδος) requires a certain ability—the capacity to "understand speech in terms of general forms, proceeding to bring many perceptions together into a reasoned unity" (*Phaedrus* 249b–c)—only a certain class of souls can enter into this kind of compound, namely, souls that have at some time in the past seen the forms, without maintaining that vision like the gods. It makes sense to refer to this class of souls as "human souls" (ἀνθρωπίνη ψυχή, 245c), but such souls can also enter lower forms of organic life. Lower souls that have never seen the forms, however, have an upper limit to the kind of organism they can enter.

This leads to a conception of the person bafflingly at odds with many contemporary assumptions yet also embedded so thoroughly in the history of philosophy that it continues to influence many of our ordinary expressions and ways of thinking about ourselves. Throughout the dialogues, the person is consistently identified with the soul rather than with the mortal organism so that speaking of "Socrates" is interchangeable with "the soul of Socrates." Not only does this alienate the body from the person, it also alienates *humanity* from the person. Socrates happens to inhabit a human being for a time, but this relationship is accidental rather than essential. In his essential state, Socrates is really a disembodied soul—a state that occupies the vast majority of his time if the various calculations of years in the myths are to be believed. To be sure, we still need to figure out how best to live the human life we are currently assigned, and this means taking seriously the question, "What does it mean to be a human being?" Nevertheless, the much more important question that Socrates asks over and over again is "What kind of thing am *I*?"—and the answer is importantly *not* "a human being."

Personalist Critique

The personalist tradition has rightly objected to all this, and it is telling how prominent the phrase "the *human* person" is in personalist writing. The personalist conception insists on viewing the person as the whole human being, who is both his body and his soul. If someone touches my hand, he has touched *me*. Even before the modern flowering of personalist philosophy, Christians have insisted since ancient times that we are human beings not temporarily and accidentally but permanently and essentially. God created us as humans, and this means that human embodiment is a good thing, so much so that, despite all empirical evidence to the contrary, Christians firmly hope for the reconstitution of this very same human body transfigured at the resurrection.

We can summarize the personalist objections to "Platonic dualism" under three points.

First, as already stated, personalists have maintained that we are essentially rather than accidentally human. When we call someone a "human person," something has misfired if we see that adjective in the same way that we see adjectives like "professional" or "friendly," signifying an optional qualification that can come and go. For most contemporary people, it is hard to grasp the full impact of the Platonic view because they find it hard to even imagine what a name like "Socrates" could refer to if not the concrete embodied human being with a famously ugly face. Just imagine what kind of a conception someone must have of himself if he thinks it is even logically possible for him to wake up one day in ten thousand years as a crab. As we will see below, however, ancient friends of Socrates had the same difficulty and several arguments in the dialogues focus precisely on opening up this conceptual space. When we alienate our humanity from ourselves in this way, we begin to see the questions of what it means to be a human being as separable from the questions of what it means to be a person. By analogy, I might currently care about what it takes to be a good accountant because I happen to be one for the time being, but I also know that my retirement is approaching in just a few years so I begin to care about it less and less. When taken to the extreme, this way of thinking can even transform into a deeply anti-human animus because our human condition comes to be seen as a hindrance to our spiritual quest to realize our true nature, often seen as a return to what we were *before* we became human. On such a view, being human looks less like temporarily being an accountant and more like being a prisoner. Such views are not hard to find in many philosophical and religious traditions ranging from varieties of Gnosticism to varieties of Hinduism, and can be found in a few of the most pessimistic passages of the *Phaedo*.

Second, since humans have a specific kind of body, divorcing my stake in humanity from my stake in myself leads to a dangerous devaluing of my relationship to my own body.[2] At one extreme, such attitudes can lead to a kind of libertinism because the deterioration of my body is not ultimately a loss to me—eat, drink, or smoke whatever you want. At the other extreme, such attitudes can lead to a perverse asceticism as I attempt to gain a total mastery of a body that I view purely as a tool wholly at the disposal of a controlling soul.

Third, personalists have objected to the way that radical dualism leads to downplaying the significance of whole domains of human experience because they are thought to derive from the "merely" physical side of our

---

2. Cf. Burgos, *Personalist Anthropology*, 50.

existence. Dietrich von Hildebrand, for example, goes to great lengths to show the damage that has been done historically by ignoring the affective dimension of human experience because affectivity was largely conceived as a *pathos* of the body.[3] Problems especially arise in the sphere of sexuality when we view our sexuality as a "mere" bodily phenomenon in opposition to the real, true, spiritual side of ourselves.[4]

The history here is complex, however, because there has been since the foundations of Christianity a mixed reaction to the Platonic picture. The early Church Fathers frequently noticed the points of fundamental disagreement such as the preexistence of the soul or cyclic reincarnation into non-human forms of life. But they also frequently noticed many points of deep affinity between the Christian conception of the person and the Platonic. As Juan Manual Burgos observes, the early Christians were impressed by the Platonic understanding of the soul because "it clearly affirmed the spirituality and immortality" of the person as well as coinciding, at least in part, with some of the self-denying ascetical practices in Christianity, such as fasting and chastity.[5]

Throughout the history of Christian devotional writing one can easily notice the imprint of this mixed beginning. We can frequently catch Christian writers, in their less careful moments, switching into a very Platonic mode of expression, speaking of the soul as though it were an independent substance and identical with the true self.[6]

At the same time that the Church Fathers were latching onto the Platonic account of the soul, widely various religious sects in the late Roman Empire were also latching on and combining Plato with numerous ideas borrowed from Babylonian, Persian, and Egyptian sources.[7] The result has been a continual stream in Western thought, which we

---

3. Dietrich von Hildebrand, *The Heart* (South Bend, IN: St. Augustine's Press, 2012).
4. See Mark K. Spencer, *The Irreducibility of the Human Person* (Washington, DC: The Catholic University of America Press, 2022), 368 ff., for a treatment of the way that many human acts, such as sexual acts, laughter, or weeping, are intrinsically both bodily and spiritual.
5. Burgos, *Personalist Anthropology*, 50.
6. By contrast, it is also worth noting that devotional writers frequently refer to their own soul in the third person, as though it had a personality of its own over and against the first-person perspective from which they are speaking.
7. Hans Jonas, *The Gnostic Religion* (Boston: Beacon Press, 1963).

can assign the convenient but often misleading label of "Gnosticism." While this stream of thought flows out of Platonism as one of its major tributaries, we must be careful here because Gnosticism is not simply identical with Platonism nor is it the logical conclusion of the Platonic model that we sketched above. Sometimes, personalist objections to "Platonic dualism" are really objections to Gnosticism, and it would be helpful to get the label right.

While "Gnosticism" was never a single, unified movement, we may identify in broad terms a few common threads that are relevant to this chapter. According to many forms of Gnosticism, the whole material cosmos functions as a kind of prison in which our divine spirits are trapped, whether from punishment, folly, or bad luck. Because the person is identified with the divine spark within (at least if one happens to belong to the elect), temporary human life along with its human body is something from which we must try to escape. Everything in the material world is to be viewed with suspicion and ultimately rejected. The traditional gods, the sun, moon, and stars, are now seen as cosmic demons or "Archons" who act as prison guards keeping us trapped. While this represents the extreme end of the anti-body attitude, more temperate versions have cropped up again and again throughout the tradition. Personalists are right, therefore, to be cautious whenever they hear dualistic talk that seems to be sliding into Gnosticism, because this slide has proved all too easy over and over again—and all too destructive.

Personalism's Debt

Without minimizing the personalist objections in the slightest, I wish to accomplish two separate but complimentary goals in this chapter. First, while one commonly hears about the Platonic dualism that "everybody knows," it is rare to find the relevant passages all in one place. By attending closely to what the dialogues actually say, side by side with one another, we can avoid the kind of broad brush strokes that so easily dismissed Plato in the last chapter.

Second, and more controversially, I hope to show that the identification of the person with the immortal soul actually serves to forward several core personalist themes in spite of the regrettable side effects that personalists are right to warn against. Consistently, the contrast between the immortal soul and the mortal human being is advanced at a moment in the dialogues where Socrates or another character wishes to separate and make vivid the opposition between our true, deep, spiritual identity and our spurious, merely conventional, social persona. The point is usually to reframe things so that we see the development of virtue as closer to our real self-interests than grasping for power, status, or pleasure. By identifying the person with the invisible soul rather than the empirically accessible human being, we are also encouraged to pursue self-knowledge through a path of interiority and dialectical reflection. This puts the notion of selfhood front and center in the ensuing Platonic tradition, and because the person is identified with an immortal soul, that selfhood is given a kind of ontological worth and dignity in the total cosmological picture that it can scarcely have for an Epicurean.

Rather than primarily advocating a hatred for the body or the material world, the whole point of the Platonic account is to get us to see ourselves as intrinsically valuable beings, beings that are immortal, responsible, and divine. Believing that I am a soul rather than a human being, a spirit whose every moral action will shape my everlasting destiny, radically shifts my way of conceptualizing myself and what is important to me. It is this radical shift in vision that lies at the heart of the Socratic paradoxes such as the dictum that it is better to suffer injustice than commit it. If I view myself in the ordinary way, this saying sounds crazy. If I view myself as a Platonic soul, however, the whole conventional value structure collapses.

In some ways, this reframing of vision lies at the very foundation of personalism's historical development. Within the Platonic tradition and its Christian Platonic descendant more than any other historical school in the West, we see a radical insistence on the intrinsic spirituality of human life, our irreducibility to empirical nature, the gravity of moral responsibility, the interior dimension of our psychic life, and the ineradicable worth of the person. All these follow from identifying the person with an immortal, divine, soul. But these desiderata come at a cost. In parallel with them we also see the development of an anti-body spirituality that historically begins to take on a life of its own and grows far more pervasive and virulent than anything we see in the dialogues.

We will expand on the importance that this spiritualization of the person has for the development of personalism in the next chapters as we examine the inner workings of the soul, the concept of νοῦς, and our relationship to the divine. For now, however, we must simply observe that the body–soul dualism in the dialogues always serves to lead us toward these very personalist themes and never merely to fixate on a hatred for the body or the material world.

Admittedly, we should not allow our agreement with the conclusions to suppress the genuine problems with the premises. At the same time, however, a critique of the basic dualism and a distaste for its later historical developments should not cause us to miss the role that the dualism actually plays in the dialogues and the debt that personalism owes historically to this whole way of thinking.

One word on historical background before we begin with the Platonic material. The metaphysical picture sketched above is frequently known as "Platonic" dualism, but Plato is hardly the originator of the idea. At about the same time as Plato, we find Isocrates drawing the same distinction between body (σῶμα) and soul (ψυχή) and holding that the soul is fit to rule, while the body is fit to be ruled. Isocrates states that such a distinction is "generally agreed" (*Antidosis* 180), so we can assume that this distinction goes back far enough to be widespread by this time.[8] Similarly, the idea of reincarnation antedates Plato. Many scholars suppose that Plato acquired this idea from Orphic or Pythagorean friends, perhaps during his stay in Sicily.[9] While this is certainly plausible, the idea also circulated widely in Greek culture during Plato's lifetime in

---

8. For translation and discussion see Long, *Greek Models of Mind and Self*, 88–93.

9. Scholars who suggest this include R. Hackforth, *Plato's Phaedo* (Cambridge: Cambridge University Press, 1955), 4; D. D. McGibbon, "The Fall of the Soul in Plato's Phaedrus," *The Classical Quarterly* 14, no. 1 (May 1964): 56–63, at 56; T. M. Robinson, *Plato's Psychology* (Toronto: University of Toronto Press, 1970), 17–18; Burger, *The Phaedo*, 7; Eva Brann, Peter Kalkavage, and Eric Salem, *Plato's Phaedo* (Franklin, TN: Focus, 1998), 3; and Long, *Greek Models of Mind and Self*, 97.

various religious and philosophical forms. Plato himself simply refers to it as an "ancient theory" (παλαιός τις λόγος) at *Phaedo* 70c and credits both "priests and priestesses" and Pindar (probably referring to his *Olympian Ode*) at *Meno* 81a–b. Plato could also find similar ideas in Empedocles or Heraclitus.[10] In all likelihood, Plato simply takes over for his own purposes a common idea that appeals to a particular religious sensibility.

Laws

We begin, perhaps wrong way round, with a heavily loaded passage from the very end of Plato's career because it so succinctly states the central issues of this chapter. In book 11 of the *Laws* the Athenian Stranger addresses a variety of laws concerning proper funeral and burial practice:

> As in other matters it is right to trust the lawgiver, so too we must believe him when he asserts that the soul is wholly superior to the body, and that in actual life what makes each of us to be what he is is nothing else than the soul (ἐν αὐτῷ τε τῷ βίῳ τὸ παρεχόμενον ἡμῶν ἕκαστον τοῦτ' εἶναι μηδὲν ἀλλ' ἢ τὴν ψυχήν), while the body is a semblance which attends on each of us (τὸ δὲ σῶμα ἰνδαλλόμενον ἡμῶν ἑκάστοις ἕπεσθαι), it being well said that the bodily corpses are images (εἴδωλα) of the dead, but that which is the real self of each of us (τὸν δὲ ὄντα ἡμῶν ἕκαστον ὄντως), and which we term the immortal soul (ἀθάνατον ψυχήν), departs to the presence of other gods, there (as the ancestral law declares) to render its account. (959a–b)[11]

Here, the Athenian Stranger uses the phrase "each of us" (ἡμῶν ἕκαστος) three times to specify the self as distinct from something else. We have two contending candidates for what "we" are: on the one hand, the body, on the other, the soul. Although we may conventionally talk about the body as though it is identical with the person, the Stranger encourages us to identify "each of us" in the strictest sense with the soul and *not*

---

10. Long, *Greek Models of Mind and Self*, 71–83.
11. Trans. R. G. Bury (Cambridge, MA: Harvard University Press, 1968). Greek text is from *Platonis Opera*, ed. John Burnet (Oxford: Oxford University Press, 1973).

with the body. Further, the inclusion of ὄντως in the phrase τὸν δὲ ὄντα ἡμῶν ἕκαστον ὄντως emphasizes a contrast between two conceptions of "each of us." On the one hand, we have what we *really* are, the *true* self. On the other hand, we have various derivative or peripheral realities that have some claim to be called "us," but are not "us" *really*.

What do we make then of the idea that the body is a "semblance" or "image" of the soul? The idea of "image," of course, contains several conceptual resonances within a Platonic context. First, someone speaking to Socrates while he is alive finds it difficult to disassociate the experience of Socrates' face from the experience of Socrates himself. Hence, he may easily mistake an experience of Socrates' body for an experience of Socrates himself just as the lovers of beautiful sights and sounds in the *Republic* mistake the images of beauty for beauty itself. When Socrates dies, however, it becomes clear that the corpse lying there at the funeral is *not* the person with whom we spoke. As the Stranger insists just after our passage,

> [t]his all goes to show that we should never squander our last penny, on the fanciful assumption that this lump of flesh being buried really is our own son or brother or whoever it is we mournfully think we are burying. (959c)[12]

We easily recognize this truth in the case of corpses—that they are only images of deceased persons—and this recognition should lead to the more difficult recognition that all along even the living bodies we experience are not the persons we know. After all, little changes about the body as it slides from living to dead. The body of Socrates is the same height before and after, it weighs just the same, and it still has a snub nose. Nevertheless, something *is* missing. "In this life," the presence of the soul furnishes the body with a dynamic vital responsiveness. That is to say, the soul furnishes "each of us to be what he is." This helps us recognize, second, that the body occupies a lower ontological station than the soul. The Stranger establishes the general priority of soul over

---

12. Trans. Saunders.

body earlier in book 10 (896a–d), but here the idea that the body is "a semblance which attends on each of us" implies this same priority in our own particular case. Third, provided that we cautiously understand the image relationship of the body to the self, the body may serve as a helpful reminder drawing our attention to a reality beyond itself: the person that the body attends as a semblance. Just as a painting of Simmias may remind Simmias's lover of Simmias himself, so too Simmias's body may serve as a reminder because it too is a "semblance" of Simmias himself.[13]

Each of Us

I want to pause for a moment to consider the careful usage of this phrase "each of us" (ἡμῶν ἕκαστος) because it is sometimes asserted that ancient Greek lacks a word for "person" or "self" and therefore lacks the concept. While it may be true that there is no single word in Greek that is consistently equivalent to our English terms, this two-word phrase does come quite close and is frequently used by Plato in important passages where he wishes to specify the person, especially when he wishes to distinguish the true or real self from the human being. In this passage, it would not do if the Stranger replaced the three instances of ἡμῶν ἕκαστος with ἄνθρωπος because the end of *human* life and the continuation of the person is just the point. As members of a biological species, humans are mortal, but "each of us" is immortal because we are identical with an immortal soul.[14]

The phrase turns up to serve a similar purpose in Aristophanes' humorous speech in the *Symposium*. Here, Aristophanes claims that each human being (ἕκαστος ἄνθρωπος) was originally a whole with two faces, four arms, and four legs (189d–e). In order to limit human power, Zeus forms the plan of cutting each human into two. Because ἄνθρωπος must refer to the whole, Aristophanes needs a term to refer to the individual that is the half, and so he reaches for ἡμῶν ἕκαστος at 191d:

13. See *Phaedo* 73d–74a.
14. See *Phaedo* 71c, 81d, discussed below.

Each of us, then, is a "matching half" of a human whole (ἕκαστος οὖν ἡμῶν ἐστιν ἀνθρώπου σύμβολον), because each was sliced like a flatfish, two out of one, and each of us is always seeking the half that matches him (ζητεῖ δὴ ἀεὶ τὸ αὑτοῦ ἕκαστος σύμβολον).[15]

In the analysis below we will see ἡμῶν ἕκαστος turn up several more times in passages that explicitly thematize the individual person as a philosophical concept.[16] Beyond these, ἡμῶν ἕκαστος occurs fourteen more times in Plato's dialogues in a sense that could reasonably be translated as "individual person," although these passages do not specifically focus on the concept.[17] In only ten instances does ἡμῶν ἕκαστος mean something that has little or nothing to do with individual personhood, for example, "each of us at the symposium."[18]

Alcibiades

Near the end of the *Alcibiades* we find a remarkable and densely packed passage directly addressing the nature of the self. Although the authorship of the *Alcibiades* is disputed, we need to examine this passage for three reasons.[19] First, this passage yields some of the most explicit evidence that a philosophical concept of personhood *is* under examination in ancient Greek philosophy. Second, it discusses explicitly and in detail the central question of this chapter. Third, the *Alcibiades* was taken to be Plato's work in Thrasyllus's list of tetralogies, and was later commented on by Iamblichus, Proclus, and Olympiodorus.[20] Insofar as we

---

15. Trans. Alexander Nehamas and Paul Woodruff.
16. *Phaedo* 95d; *Republic* 369b, 370a–b, 435e, 441d; *Laws* 626e–627a, 644c, d, 687e, 904c.
17. *Theaetetus* 166c, d, 178e; *Philebus* 38a, 40a; *Phaedrus* 237d; *Gorgias* 497b, c, 507d; *Meno* 72a; *Republic* 344e, 618c; *Laws* 807b, 895d.
18. *Statesman* 177d; *Philebus* 17b; *Symposium* 177d, 198e; *Charmides* 155c, 172d; *Laches* 194d; *Laws* 642b, 699d, 838c.
19. For arguments in favor of Platonic authorship, see Annas, "Self Knowledge in Early Plato," 111–38; David M. Johnson, "God as the True Self: Plato's Alcibiades i," *Ancient Philosophy* 19 (1999): 1–19; *Plato: Alcibiades*, ed. Nicholas Denyer (Cambridge: Cambridge University Press, 2001). Nicholas D. Smith, "Did Plato Write the Alcibiades i?" *Apeiron* 37, no. 2 (2004), 93–108, argues against. For a good review of the scholarship on the issue see Smith, "Did Plato Write the Alcibiades i?" 94 n. 6.
20. See Annas, "Self Knowledge in Early Plato," 112 n. 5, for a list of references throughout multiple philosophical schools in antiquity.

are investigating the availability of ideas for later thinkers, the real authorship of the dialogue is immaterial. Later thinkers read the ideas in the *Alcibiades* as Platonic whether Plato really wrote it or not.

The best material on the person comes at the end of the dialogue in two sections, 129a–131d and 132d–133c. I will address the first of these sections here because it deals explicitly with the relationships between body, soul, and person. The second section is a much debated passage relating the true or highest self to the divine, which I have treated at length elsewhere.[21] From the first section, I want to draw out two central ideas. First, Socrates specifies the self contrastively by using the familiar concepts of owning and using. The self is the owner *in contrast to* the thing owned and the user *in contrast to* the thing used. These two contrasts historically provide two of the core metaphors for thinking about the person, metaphors that have become so commonplace that we often forget they are metaphors at all. Second, Socrates advances an argument by elimination showing that the self is identical to the soul rather than the body or the soul–body composite. This argument is important because it is one of the only places in all the dialogues where an explicit argument is presented for this conclusion. Elsewhere, arguments to this effect may by subtly implied, but more usually the identity of the soul and the person is simply asserted as a premise in a larger argument advancing the Socratic project of virtue and self-knowledge.

The bulk of the dialogue leading up to our passage aims at convincing Alcibiades that he needs to practice self-cultivation. Quoting the Delphic Inscription, Socrates persuades Alcibiades that self-cultivation requires self-knowledge (124a–b). We need to know what we are before we can specify what the art of self-cultivation is.

Socrates begins by drawing a distinction between owner and possession. He asks, "[I]s [a man] cultivating himself when he cultivates what he has?"[22] The skill of shoemaking, for instance, looks after shoes rather than feet so it looks after what belongs to the feet rather than the

---

21. D. T. Sheffler, "Is the True Self God at *Alcibiades* 133c?" *The International Journal of the Platonic Tradition* (June 2022).

22. All translations from the *Alcibiades* are from D. S. Hutchinson.

feet themselves. This means that "when you're cultivating what belongs to you, you're not cultivating yourself" (128d). Ruling out a whole class of skills that do not count as self-cultivation, Socrates reintroduces his central question:

> What sort of skill could we use to cultivate ourselves? ... [I]t's a skill that won't make anything that belongs to us better, but it will make *us* better.... Well then, could we ever know what skill makes us better if we didn't know what *we* were (τί ποτ' ἐσμὲν αὐτοί)? (128e)

The question "What are *we*?" must be answered in contrast to "What *belongs* to us?" This puts the inquiry into the nature of the self within the conceptual framework of ownership. Alongside the owner–possession pair Socrates next employs the user–tool pair:

> Hold on, by Zeus—who are you speaking with now? Anybody but me? ... Is Socrates doing the talking? ... And isn't Socrates talking with words? ... I suppose you'd say that talking is the same as using words? ... But the thing being used and the person using it—they're different, aren't they (ὁ δὲ χρώμενος καὶ ᾧ χρῆται οὐκ ἄλλο)? (129a–c)

Here Socrates returns to shoemaking and draws a distinction between the shoemaker and his knife because the one *uses* the other. Again, in the same way that he first orients the conversation in terms of owning something, he now orients it in terms of using something.

Separating owner from thing owned and user from thing used both aim at bringing Alcibiades to a basic apprehension of the self as an object of inquiry. Alcibiades can begin with something familiar to him, like speaking, and from there distinguish the user (himself) from what he uses (the words). He may begin with a conventional sense that his words are him, but Socrates' considerations cause both *that which belongs to Alcibiades* and *that which Alcibiades uses* to appear external to the *real* or *true* Alcibiades. As a byproduct of this technique—perhaps an intentional one—readers of the dialogue are encouraged to think about the nature of the true self primarily in terms of possessions and tools. This is significant because both possessions and tools are ways that agents extend their agency. By *having* more leather, the shoemaker can make more shoes. By *using* a knife, the shoemaker can cut leather that he could not cut before. This orients our conception of the self in terms of power and its extension.

This becomes especially important as Socrates extends his analysis to the body. Besides the knife, the shoemaker also uses his hands and eyes (129d). Thus, "the shoemaker and the lyre player are different from the hands and eyes they use in their work" (129d). Although the knife is separable from the shoemaker in a way that his hand is not, the shoemaker uses this part of himself as an instrument to accomplish his tasks. In an ordinary sense, we naturally think of the hand as the person. For instance, if someone touches Alcibiades' hand, then he is touching Alcibiades. If my hand is holding a glass, then *I* am holding it. By considering Socrates' comparison between knife-as-tool and hand-as-tool, however, Alcibiades' hand appears less and less to be him and more and more to be something that his real self merely uses. This is an enormously consequential pivot point in the way that we think about the relationship between person, self, and body—a point that personalists contest. Perhaps the ever-wily Socrates wants Alcibiades to contest this all-too-easy analogy between knife and hand, but the impetuous youth simply goes along with the stream of deductions.

What goes for the hand also goes for the eyes and presumably the feet and ears as well. Socrates draws an inference, therefore, from all the parts to the whole: "man uses his whole body" (παντὶ τῷ σώματι χρῆται ἄνθρωπος). Therefore, "a man is different from his own body" (ἕτερον ἄρα ἄνθρωπός ἐστι τοῦ σώματος τοῦ ἑαυτοῦ, 129e). Hence, although we naturally associate the body with the activities of the person, the body is merely the extension of the *real* person's agency. The body *belongs to* the person and *is used by* the person, so it must be distinct from the person that *has* and *uses*.

This leads Socrates to reintroduce the question from 128e in slightly different terms. There he asks, "What are we?" (τί ποτ᾽ ἐσμὲν αὐτοί). Here he asks, "What is man?" (τί ποτ᾽ οὖν ὁ ἄνθρωπος, 129e). He insists that Alcibiades already knows the answer to this question despite his protests. The "man" must be "what uses the body," and nothing else uses the body but the soul. In fact, the soul not only uses the body but rules it (ἄρχουσα, 130a). Interestingly, this conception of the soul as the ruler and user of the body is taken for granted as a premise and inserted into the reasoning as something that Alcibiades should already know. Perhaps this reflects the already pervasive acceptance of these categories that we saw also in the saying of Isocrates.

Although his previous comments already seem to provide a conclusion, Socrates abruptly begins a new argument. I suspect that he starts fresh because the brevity of the move in 130a may appear to beg the question. That is, we would think that the soul uses and rules the body only if we already think of the soul as the true person. Whatever his motives may be, Socrates next presents a three-pronged argument from elimination for the conclusion that the soul is the person or "man."

1. Man is one of three things (130a): (a) the body, (b) the soul, or (c) the two of them together, the "whole thing."
2. Man is that which rules the body (cf. 129e).
3. The body does not rule itself (130b).
4. If one of them (that is, body or soul) does not take part in ruling, then no combination of the two could rule (130b).
5. Therefore, the soul must be the man (130c).

This argument results in the dictum "the soul is the man" (ἡ ψυχή ἐστιν ἄνθρωπος, 130c).

Beginning with his distinction between user and thing used and continuing through this argument from elimination, Socrates introduces ἄνθρωπος ("man") as the key term where earlier he simply said "we" (128e) or "the self" (129a). I think Hutchinson's translation of ἄνθρωπος here as "man" is slightly better than "human" because the latter encourages us to think of a biological species (as in the *Phaedo*, see below). In fact, in the rest of the corpus, Plato consistently uses ἄνθρωπος to refer to the mortal biological animal that *we* are only for a time. We saw this usage already in the passage from the *Symposium* describing the funny beings of Aristophanes' tale, and we will see it again multiple times in the *Phaedo* and the *Phaedrus* below. The anomalous declaration that ἡ ψυχή ἐστιν ἄνθρωπος, therefore, counts as one small point against genuine authorship. But it may also reflect an early phase of Plato's way of speaking about such things because the argument makes exactly the same point, if expressed in slightly different words, as all the other passages that use ἄνθρωπος to refer to the mortal composite whole.

When Socrates especially wants to specify the true person he shifts away from using ἄνθρωπος to using the proper names "Socrates" and "Alcibiades" (for example, 129a). This serves a double function. First, it helps Alcibiades identify the object of inquiry in the immediate space of conversation. Rather than considering the abstraction "Man," he focuses on the immediate person, Socrates, who addresses him directly. Second, it serves Socrates' ultimate goal of persuading Alcibiades that no one else loves *him*. All his other lovers only love what Alcibiades *has*, while Socrates loves *him* (131c–d). This appeal would lose some of its force if Alcibiades did not from the first consider the distinction between true person and externals in terms of "Alcibiades" and "Socrates." We see this most clearly when Socrates sums up what they have discovered together:

> So the right way of looking at it is that, when you and I talk to each other, one soul uses words to address another soul (τοῖς λόγοις χρωμένους τῇ ψυχῇ πρὸς τὴν ψυχήν).… That's just what we were saying a little while ago—that Socrates converses with Alcibiades not by saying words to his face, apparently, but by addressing his words to *Alcibiades*, in other words, to his soul. (130d–e)

This passage is an especially striking example of the way that, from the very beginning of the Western philosophical tradition, personalist themes have been rooted first and foremost in the conceptual space of I–Thou encounter and conversation, rather than exclusively in terms of solitary introspection.

Phaedo

The *Phaedo* forms the center of the anti-body dualism that "everybody knows." It is short enough to be read in a freshmen philosophy class, and its moving depiction of Socrates in his final moments have captivated generations of readers. The centrality of this dialogue to the Platonic doctrine of soul and body therefore requires that we devote the longest section of this chapter to a careful examination of the text. Rather than picking anti-body statements out of context, we must recognize the rhetorical purpose for which they are employed. Socrates seeks to reassure his friends that his death is not a catastrophe, that he instead has a justifiable hope that his soul will go on to a better condition. Taking this rhetorical context into account, however, we must also face honestly the sometimes extreme anti-body position that is articulated (whether Socrates ultimately, secretly, in his heart of hearts means it or not).[23]

Near the beginning of the *Phaedo* Socrates alludes to a doctrine "put in the language of the mysteries, that we men are in a kind of prison" (ἔν τινι φρουρᾷ ἐσμεν οἱ ἄνθρωποι, 62b).[24] Socrates interprets this to mean that the prison we are in is the body and our soul is forced to "examine other things through it as through a cage and not by itself" (82e).

This picture leads him to the first section of serious argument, which runs from 63e to 69e. Here, Socrates delivers a second "apology" to his friends the "jury" in defense of the good hope he has facing death. In the *Apology* proper, Socrates argued that fear in the face of death is irrational because we have no way of knowing, one way or the other, whether what awaits us is fearful. Here, however, he argues to his friends that he has solid reasons for thinking that death will bring him to a better condition. The first phase of this argument runs from 64c to 68c and ends with the striking conclusion that the proper aim of philosophy is "to practice for dying and death." We can summarize the argument as follows:

23. Cf. the secret-decoder-ring reading of Socrates cited above in Burger, *The Phaedo*.
24. Unless otherwise noted, all translations from the *Phaedo* are taken from G. M. A. Grube. Note that ἔν τινι φρουρᾷ may also mean "in a kind of guardhouse." Burger, *The Phaedo*, 33, believes that this ambiguity is intentional, contrasting the human philosopher's perspective that desires to escape from the body and the divine perspective that assigns the soul to the body and prohibits suicide.

1. Death is "the separation of the soul from the body" (64c).
2. The philosopher concerns himself with the affairs of the soul rather than the body (64c–65a) because:
   a. The body is an obstacle and deceives the soul in the pursuit of knowledge (65a–b).
   b. The soul reasons best when it is untroubled by the body and its senses (65c–66a).
   c. This is because we cannot grasp the forms through the senses, but only by thought alone (65d–e).
3. Therefore, the philosopher seeks to separate the soul as far as possible from the body (66a–66d).
4. Full separation of the soul from the body is only possible after death (66e–67d, cf. Premise 1).
5. Therefore, true philosophers welcome that which brings the fulfillment of their main preoccupation (67d–68c).

Every step in the argument depends on Socrates' initial definition of death as "the separation of the soul from the body." He immediately expands this definition with a more precise formula:

> Death is this, namely, that the body comes to be separated by itself apart from the soul (χωρὶς μὲν ἀπὸ τῆς ψυχῆς ἀπαλλαγὲν αὐτὸ καθ᾽ αὑτὸ τὸ σῶμα γεγονέναι), and the soul comes to be separated by itself apart from the body (χωρὶς δὲ τὴν ψυχὴν ἀπὸ τοῦ σώματος ἀπαλλαγεῖσαν αὐτὴν καθ᾽ αὑτὴν εἶναι). (64c)[25]

Right away, the careful reader of Plato should notice the deliberate usage of αὐτὸ καθ᾽ αὑτό, which occurs frequently in descriptions of the forms (for example, below at 66a). This phrase occurs particularly in conjunction with the notion of being "separate" (χωρίς) at *Parmenides* 130b, terminology that will become central to centuries of debate between the Platonic school and their Aristotelian friends. This separability brings with it an epistemic dimension as well. Only when the soul is αὐτὴ καθ᾽

---

25. Compare this with a very similar definition at *Gorgias* 524b.

αὐτήν is it in a position to come into contact with the forms as they are αὐτὸ καθ' αὐτό in premises 2b and 2c.

Next, Socrates establishes (premise 2) that the body prevents or at least hinders "the actual acquiring of knowledge" (τῆς φρονήσεως κτῆσιν, 65a) when the soul "grasp[s] the truth" (τῆς ἀληθείας ἅπτεται, 65b). The body systematically opposes knowledge and understanding by (i) causing the soul to desire bodily things like food and sex (64d–e), (ii) distracting the soul with the constant reports of sensation (65c), and (iii) deceiving the soul through the inherent unreliability of sense perception (65a–e). Socrates concludes from this that the soul must be as free as possible from this opposition and distraction if it is to achieve any true understanding. The soul does this best when it is "most by itself" (μάλιστα αὐτὴ καθ' αὑτήν, 65c). This leads Socrates to a hortatory speech exemplary of what philosophers must assert to one another in order to keep up their confidence at the prospect of death (66b–67a).

Throughout, we should notice a basic asymmetry in the way that Socrates talks about body and soul. Socrates pairs the opposition between body and soul with an opposition between sense perception and reasoning. Because the philosopher "turns away from the body toward the soul" (64e) one might expect that the philosopher accomplishes sense perception through the body and reasoning through the soul. We do not, however, find this symmetry. The soul is the single subject of both sense perception and reason, although it does require a body for sense perception. Hence, the soul is conceived as the conscious subject, experiencing pure thought when it is undisturbed by the body but experiencing sense perception "through" the body in our present, annoying condition.[26]

Next, Socrates advances a series of arguments that seem questionable, not just to generations of readers, but to the interlocutors in the dialogue itself. Unfortunately, we will not have occasion to examine the precise causes of the arguments' questionable nature. Here, we will simply focus on the way that Socrates consistently uses ἄνθρωπος to mean "a human

---

26. Sabina Lovibond, "Plato's Theory of Mind," in *Psychology*, ed. Stephen Everson (Cambridge: Cambridge University Press, 1991), 35–55, at 35–36, argues that Plato in fact *invents* the idea of the conscious subject and expands the meaning of ψυχή to include it.

being" in the sense of a mortal biological organism belonging to the human species, distinct from the person who may happen to belong to the species for a time. Surprisingly, at least to modern readers, *this* aspect of the reasoning goes entirely unquestioned by the interlocutors despite their careful objections to several other points. This may reflect a background set of Pythagorean and Orphic assumptions, since several of the named interlocutors, especially Cebes and Simmias, are noted Pythagoreans.[27]

The definition of death at 64c requires that both the body and the soul continue to exist as separate substances, and Socrates takes this as a basic premise in his Second Apology. Cebes, however, says that accepting this premise requires a "good deal of faith and persuasive argument." For Cebes, it is not completely apparent that

> [t]he soul still exists after a man has died (ἀποθανόντος τοῦ ἀνθρώπου) and that it still possesses some capability and intelligence (καί τινα δύναμιν ἔχει καὶ φρόνησιν). (70b)

In the middle section of the *Phaedo*, therefore, Socrates proceeds to offer "a good deal of persuasive argument" for just this conclusion. We must be careful to note, however, what Cebes requires Socrates to establish. First, Socrates must argue that the soul continues to exist when a human being dies. Second, Socrates must argue that the soul that survives must continue to possess "some capability and intelligence." Hence, the famous argument for immortality in the *Phaedo* takes its point of departure from a major and a minor concern. The major concern is obvious: What if nothing survives death? The minor concern is less obvious but still important: What if *something* survives, but it lacks agency (δύναμις) and intelligence (φρόνησις)?[28]

---

27. It is difficult to say just how much of this picture belongs to a historical Pythagorean school and how much is introduced by Plato himself since the evidence for the content of Pythagoreanism in this period is so sparse and the testimony of later authors is so heavily mixed with Platonism, frequently drawing on the *Phaedo* itself.

28. David Bostock, *Plato's Phaedo* (Oxford: Oxford University Press, 1986), 25, paraphrases Cebes' requirement as the requirement that the disembodied soul remain "conscious and active." Lloyd Gerson, *Knowing Persons*, 51, thinks that the conception of the immortal soul in the *Phaedo* ideally involves "self-reflexive cognition." It seems to me that the constraint of φρόνησιν ἔχειν requires only cognition *simpliciter*, especially cognition of the Forms.

Suppose that a vaporous, smoky substance called "the soul" does survive death, floating off on the breeze.[29] Suppose this substance does not think or perceive anything at all, and differs from the blood and bones of the body only in its rarity. On this picture, the soul continues to exist but is *just stuff*. What is wrong with this kind of survival? Why does Cebes need to add the continued possession of "capability and intelligence" to the list of things that Socrates must show? In a general sense, we can see the hopelessness of this picture. The survival of dumb stuff—call it "soul" if you like—simply does not amount to the survival of Socrates any more than the survival of his bones in the grave. There is, however, a more specific sense in which the survival of dumb stuff proves inadequate in the terms of Socrates' own Second Apology. Philosophers ought to have confidence in the face of death, says Socrates, because they have oriented their lives toward the pursuit of knowledge, a pursuit that the body constantly hampers. Only after death does the soul become free from the constraints of the body and thereby gain wisdom (φρόνησις, 66a, see also 79d). Should the soul survive without possessing "capability and intelligence," the hope that death brings knowledge would be futile. Should death transform the philosopher into a dumb vapor, death would turn out to be worse for philosophy than embodied human life and the justification for Socrates' hopeful expectation would fall apart. This reasoning remains essentially the same when we consider other, less materialistic pictures of survival. Suppose, for instance, that we all survive by merging with a single, cosmic World Soul. As long as this condition does not involve the continued possession of intelligence on the part of *the philosopher*, it will not serve to justify Socrates' confidence in the face of death.[30]

Socrates responds to Cebes's objection with the so-called Cyclical

---

29. Something like this view seems to be held by Homer. See Long, *Greek Models of Mind and Self*, chapter 1, and W. K. C. Guthrie, *The Greek Philosophers* (New York: Harper Perennial, 1960), 30–31.

30. Mary Margaret McCabe, *Plato's Individuals* (Princeton, NJ: Princeton University Press, 1994), 264: "[Socrates's friends] are afraid that by the next day there will be no more Socrates (not no more souls). So it would hardly be consolation to them to show, for example, that the form of soul is deathless. Plato must demonstrate that Socrates' soul is immortal, that we go on and on as individuals, not as a generic soul, or even as part of some reservoir of psychic stuff."

Argument and Recollection Argument. The Cyclical Argument focuses on establishing the substantial existence of the soul before and after human embodiment (Cebes's major concern), while the Recollection Argument focuses on establishing the intellectual capacity of the soul in its disembodied state (Cebes' minor concern). For our purposes, we can pass over the short and somewhat quizzical Cyclical Argument (70d–72e) except to say that it both presupposes and reinforces the picture sketched above: A person is soul; the soul exists before birth and after death, belonging to a population of souls that Socrates calls "the dead"; between birth and death, while conjoined to a human body, that person happens to be a human being and belongs to the population called "the living." The terminology here stands in tension with the later arguments that Socrates advances to show that souls must necessarily be "living" by their very essence. The picture, however, of the person as a soul that is merely temporarily human remains constant throughout.

After Socrates advances this argument, Cebes reminds Socrates of the theory of recollection. This theory is introduced by Plato in the *Meno* in what many scholars conclude is an earlier dialogue. There, the theory is explained by way of the famous demonstration of the Pythagorean theorem by the slave boy, but the metaphysical underpinnings of the theory are left somewhat thin. Perhaps Cebes' "reminder" here is Plato's way of referencing the *Meno* and signaling both its applicability to the immortality of the soul and his desire to explain the theory of recollection in more robust terms. Cebes says that, according to this theory,

> [w]e must at some previous time have learned what we now recollect. This is possible only if our soul existed somewhere before it took on this human shape (ἦν που ἡμῖν ἡ ψυχὴ πρὶν ἐν τῷδε τῷ ἀνθρωπίνῳ εἴδει γενέσθαι). So according to this theory too, the soul is likely to be something immortal. (72e–73a)

Simmias says that he is a little fuzzy on the details of this theory so Socrates explains it. In brief, it is impossible for us to *come to know* the forms in this life but we are nevertheless *reminded* of them. For a reminder to work, one must already know the thing remembered. Hence, *we* must have come to know before this life begins what *we* remember now. While this argument does not say anything directly about the condition of the soul after death, it does say much about the possibility of an intelligent mode of being for us apart from human embodiment. If we knew the forms before we were born, we should be able to know them again after we die.

We see this point especially in the way that Socrates sums up the conclusion of the Recollection Argument:

> When did our souls acquire knowledge of them [that is, the forms]? Certainly not since we were born as men (ἄνθρωποι γεγόναμεν).... So then, Simmias, our souls also existed apart from the body before they took on human form, and they had intelligence (ἦσαν ἄρα, ὦ Σιμμία, αἱ ψυχαὶ καὶ πρότερον, πρὶν εἶναι ἐν ἀνθρώπου εἴδει, χωρὶς σωμάτων, καὶ φρόνησιν εἶχον). (76c)

If we grant its premises, the Recollection Argument certainly establishes the existence of the soul before birth—one must exist in order to learn—but the real focus of the argument rests on the intelligent nature of the soul's disembodied state: it had knowledge of the forms. This recalls the description of φρόνησις as a "state" (πάθημα) of the soul that has come to be "alone by itself" (αὐτὴ καθ' αὑτήν) apprehending the forms (79d).

Simmias also speaks of the soul "existing before it enters a human body" (πρὶν καὶ εἰς ἀνθρώπειον σῶμα ἀφικέσθαι, 77b), and Socrates echoes this same language later at 95c–d when he speaks of the soul as existing "before we were born as men" (πρὶν ἡμᾶς ἀνθρώπους γενέσθαι) and its "entrance into a human body" (τὸ εἰς ἀνθρώπου σῶμα ἐλθεῖν).

Twice in this discussion we see the word "shape" (εἶδος), indicating the structure of the human organism. We do not have soul and body jumbled together in any old way but, rather, soul and body join together in a specific configuration set by the nature of a human being. In both cases, the theory of recollection establishes that the soul exists prior to its union with "this human shape." This makes clear that we are not reading Aristotle (or St. Thomas for that matter), for whom the soul *is* the form of the living organism. Instead the soul undergoes a process of entering into this human shape, and this process marks the beginning of a human life. Notice, also, that the body is not the human being any more than the soul is. The individual human is instead the composite formed by soul and body together.[31] The soul exists both before and after this union in some other mode, while the material that constitutes the body also continues to exist separately for a time (χωρίς, cf. 64c).

More than the other arguments, the Recollection Argument aims at the individual thinking person, and this makes sense given that its subject matter is memory. When I remember something, I never remember the prior experiences of another mind. The knowledge I recall is always the knowledge *I* previously learned. In our present human life, Socrates grounds our recognition that these particular sticks are equal in knowledge of the equal itself prior to human life (74e–75c). Because we could not have gained this knowledge at any time during our human embodiment, we must have gained it before *we* entered "this human shape."

We face a twist, however, because each person remembers the same thing: the equal and its like, which must be both objective and universal. Hence, the kind of memory under examination is not the episodic and idiosyncratic kind that becomes so important for Locke's theory of personal identity. We have nothing—in this passage at any rate—that would *qualitatively* differentiate one person from another, but it does not follow from this that Cebes and Socrates are *numerically* identical before birth. We should be careful, therefore, not to confuse two distinct issues. On the one hand, we have "person" in the sense of "personality," the source of unique flair and genius, so beloved by Romantic thinkers such as Goethe or von Humboldt. On the other hand, we have "person" in the sense of "individual substance of a rational nature," a numerically singular mind capable of knowledge. The memory at issue in the Recollection

---

31. This analysis also makes good sense of what Socrates says at *Phaedrus* 246c: "A soul that sheds its wings wanders until it lights on something solid, where it settles and takes on an earthly body, which then, owing to the power of this soul, seems to move itself. The whole combination of soul and body is called a living thing (ζῷον τὸ σύμπαν ἐκλήθη, ψυχὴ καὶ σῶμα παγέν), or animal, and has the designation 'mortal' as well. Such a combination cannot be immortal, not on any reasonable account" (all translations from the *Phaedrus* are from Alexander Nehamas and Paul Woodruff).

Argument is "impersonal" in the first sense, but it need not be in the second.³² This gives us further insight into the way that Socrates is implicitly conceiving the individual self. If (i) the Socrates who now remembers is the same person as the Socrates who formerly knew before birth and (ii) there is nothing qualitatively unique about this connection, then personal identity must not depend on the idiosyncratic features of embodied life. Instead, personal identity would depend on a numerically singular and, at some level, continuous act of apprehending the equal and its like because this act is all that links Socrates then and Socrates now.

It is important that the recollection argument establishes this individual and intelligent nature of the soul's disembodied state because the other arguments only lightly touch on this. Taken apart from the Recollection Argument, therefore, we may suspect that these arguments are discussing something other than the individual, intelligent person when they discuss "the soul." We should read the arguments together, however, rather than apart. Taken in this way, the other arguments rely on the Recollection Argument to establish the individual, intelligent nature of the disembodied soul and continue to have this conception in view throughout. We see this conception surface again when Socrates summarizes Cebes' "Second Objection" (that Socrates has only proven that the soul continues after death, not that it is forever immortal):

> You say it makes no difference whether [the soul] enters a body once or many times as far as the fear of each of us is concerned (πρός γε τὸ ἕκαστον ἡμῶν φοβεῖσθαι), for it is natural for a man who is no fool to be afraid, if he does not know and cannot prove that the soul is immortal. (95d)

---

32. Hackforth, *Plato's Phaedo*, 75: "In default of recollection of personal experience it is difficult to see how there can be that consciousness of identity preserved through a series of incarnations without which one cannot properly speak of individual immortality." Both Hackforth and Bostock, *Plato's Phaedo*, 36, think that *personal* immortality requires unique episodic memory, but they do not consider the distinction I draw here. In my view, McCabe, *Plato's Individuals*, 265–66, and Gerson, *Knowing Persons*, 10, 23, 193, 279, get this right. Gerson, *Knowing Persons*, 279: "A multitude of disembodied knowers, however, each knowing the same things, does not in principle seem to be a contradiction."

Although, the dialogue has shifted to a concern for full-blown immortality rather than temporary survival after death, the concern still motivating the discussion is the "fear of each of us" (again note the important usage of the phrase ἕκαστος ἡμῶν). Establishing temporary survival is not enough to handle the party's fear *for Socrates*.

Again we see a separation between the individual person considered as an individual soul and the individual human being when Socrates advances the Kinship Argument. Over the course of the argument, Socrates establishes several pairs of contrasting opposites. At each step, Socrates asks Cebes to assign both the soul and the body to the pairs. This culminates at 80b when Socrates gathers up all the pairs side by side, with the soul in one half and the body in the other:

Soul (ψυχή)	Body (σῶμα)
Divine (θεῖος)	Human (ἀνθρώπινος)
Deathless (ἀθάνατος)	Mortal (θνητός)
Intelligible (νοητός)	Unintelligible (ἀνόητος)
Uniform (μονοειδής)	Multiform (πολυειδής)
Indissoluble (ἀδιάλυτος)	Soluble (διαλυτός)
Always the same as itself	Never consistently the same

Most striking for our concerns is the appearance of "human" (ἀνθρώπινος) on the side of the body and the appearance of "divine" (θεῖος) on the side of the soul. In the Recollection Argument, the soul appeared as something merely different from the individual human because it had some mode of existence prior to this human life. Here, however, Socrates describes the soul specifically *in opposition to* what is human. Mortality and unintelligibility are proper to the human sphere. During its time in "this human shape" such qualities may afflict the soul, but they do so always as outside invaders. In its own right, the soul is divine *rather than* human and possesses immortality and intelligibility as proper to its own nature. This confronts the soul with the ethical task of casting off as far as possible these alien features that come along with human embodiment. Hence, the good soul makes its way to what is like itself, the "divine" and "immortal," having freed itself "of various human ills" (τῶν ἄλλων κακῶν τῶν ἀνθρωπείων, 81a).

Again, Socrates simply speaks of "the soul" throughout the Opposites Argument, and the examples of snow and fire certainly encourage us to think about generic, homogeneous stuff, but he summarizes the conclusion of the argument thus:

> Therefore the soul, Cebes, he said, is most certainly deathless and indestructible and our souls will really dwell in the underworld. (106e–107a)

Notice, then, how Socrates switches from "the soul" in the singular to "our souls" in the plural. All along, the abstract discussion about "the soul" has direct implications for Socrates and his friends. After all, "not even a comic poet," Socrates says, "could say that I am babbling and discussing things that do not concern me."[33]

After offering all these arguments in the mode of his customary dialectic, Socrates switches into the long telling of a striking afterlife myth. While it differs in the details, the general picture and especially the spirit of the myth echoes similar afterlife myths in the *Gorgias*, *Republic*, and *Phaedrus* (discussed below). We can divide the *Phaedo* myth into three main sections. The first gives some general remarks on the fate of souls being led by guides after death (107d–108c). The second gives a long aside on the true nature of the earth, complete with a description of the various channels that run in and out of Tartarus (108c–113c). The third relies upon this portrayal of the earth's structure to give further details on the journeys of the dead (113d–115a).

Turning to the very beginning of the myth we notice the point, running throughout, that Socrates seeks to establish not just "immortality of the soul" but continuity of the conscious person:

---

33. *Phaedo* 70c. Peter J. Ahrensdorf, *The Death of Socrates and the Life of Philosophy: An Interpretation of Plato's Phaedo* (Albany: State University of New York Press, 1995), 87–88, is therefore unjustified in drawing a hard distinction between talk of "the soul" and "our souls" in the Cyclical Argument. Richard Sorabji, *Self*, 115, is also incorrect to say, "As regards soul, Plato himself speaks as if all soul is one, indivisible except amongst bodies." See Bostock, *Plato's Phaedo*, 187, for the absurdity of this interpretation of the *Phaedo*.

> If death were escape from everything, it would be a great boon to the wicked to get rid of the body and of their wickedness together with their soul. But now that the soul appears to be immortal, there is no escape from evil or salvation for it except by becoming as good and wise as possible, for the soul goes to the underworld possessing nothing but its education and upbringing, which are said to bring the greatest benefit or harm to the dead right at the beginning of the journey yonder. (107c–d)

The hypothesis that Socrates rejects, "if death were escape from everything," turns on the destruction of both body and soul. This would turn out wonderfully for the wicked because they can "get rid" of both their body and soul and hence escape any lasting consequences for their wickedness by simply slipping into nonexistence. Socrates rejects this hypothesis, however, in favor of the idea that we cannot escape the condition of our souls because those souls are immortal. I should act in the long-term interests of my soul because I *am* that soul.[34]

Finally, we should say something about the notion of rebirth present in the myth. This will receive fuller treatment in the *Phaedrus* and *Republic*, but we find it already in the *Phaedo*. The fates of various souls differ in terms of where they go, how long they stay, and whether or not they will be reborn.

> [The Acheron] flows through many other deserted regions and further underground makes its way to the Acherusian lake to which the souls of the majority come after death and, after remaining there for a certain appointed time, longer for some, shorter for others, they are sent back to birth as living creatures (πάλιν ἐκπέμπονται εἰς τὰς τῶν ζῴων γενέσεις). (113a)

The term "living creatures" implies that rebirth is not limited to rebirth as humans. Indeed, earlier in the dialogue, Socrates says that souls are reborn into bodies because of their longing for the physical, and they are then "bound to such characters as they have practiced in their life" (81e). He enumerates a few possibilities: first, the gluttonous and drunk

---

34. Long, *Greek Models of Mind and Self*, 54: "In these [Platonic myths] the postmortem *psyche* is no senseless ghost. It is the bodiless but mentally and morally complete survivor of the previously embodied person."

become donkeys or similar animals; second, the unjust and tyrannous become wolves, hawks, and kites; and third, those who have practiced "popular and social virtue" but "without philosophy or understanding" become gregarious animals such as bees, wasps, ants, or "the same kind of human group" (ταὐτόν γε πάλιν τὸ ἀνθρώπινον γένος). Once again, therefore, we have the idea that diverse lives lead to diverse individual fates and the idea that this should motivate the pursuit of a philosophical life (82a–b, see also the allotment of fates in the myth at 113d–114b).

After the myth and just before he is about to drink the hemlock, Socrates expresses his last wishes saying, "[T]ake good care of your own selves (ὑμῶν αὐτῶν ἐπιμελούμενοι) in whatever you do." Crito responds, "We shall be eager to follow your advice ... but how shall we bury you?" Interpreted literally, Crito's question implies that *Socrates* will still be around to bury after he dies, and Socrates exploits this literal interpretation to make a joke with a serious point:

> [You may bury me] in any way you like, said Socrates, if you can catch me and I do not escape you. And laughing quietly, looking at us, he said: I do not convince Crito that I am this Socrates talking to you here and ordering all I say, but he thinks that I am the thing which we will soon be looking at as a corpse, and so he asks how he shall bury me. I have been saying for some time and at some length that after I have drunk the poison I shall no longer be with you but will leave you to go and enjoy some good fortunes of the blessed, but it seems that I have said all this to him in vain in an attempt to reassure you and myself too. Give a pledge to Crito on my behalf, he said, the opposite pledge to that he gave the jury. He pledged that I would stay; you must pledge that I will not stay after I die, but that I shall go away, so that Crito will bear it more easily when he sees my body being burned or buried and will not be angry on my behalf, as if I were suffering terribly, and so that he should not say at the funeral that he is laying out or carrying out or burying Socrates. For know you well, my dear Crito, that to express oneself badly is not only faulty as far as the language goes, but does some harm to the soul. You must be of good cheer, and say you are burying my body, and bury it in any way you like and think most customary. (115c–116a)

Socrates' own words suggest that we should look carefully at this passage because here we find in summary what Socrates has been "saying for some time and at some length." If the identity between soul and self were not operative throughout the dialogue, Socrates would have no hope—and no joke.

Gorgias

Although the account at the end of the *Gorgias* bears all the features of a myth, Socrates calls it "a very fine account" (μάλα καλὸς λόγος) as opposed to a "mere tale" (μῦθος), something he will relate "as true" (ὡς ἀληθῆ, 523a).[35] He tells the story of a divine law "concerning human beings" that determines where they go after death: the just and pious to the Isles of the Blessed and the unjust and godless to the "prison of payment and retribution" (523b). While there is nothing wrong with this law itself, there was a problem with its administration during the reign of Chronus: Living judges judged living men (523b). This meant that the judges were inaccurately determining who was just and who was unjust, and hence, they sent people to the wrong places. Zeus corrects this injustice by making three important changes: (i) the judgment takes place after death without the individual knowing when it is coming, (ii) both judges and judged are stripped naked, and (iii) the judgment is given to three of Zeus's trusted sons, with the third being an arbiter in difficult cases.

The most important of these changes for the argument in the *Gorgias* is (ii). According to Zeus, the judgments go awry because the judges are apt to countenance illegitimate and extraneous things in their judgments:

> The cases are being badly decided at this time because those being judged are judged fully dressed. They're being judged while they're still alive. Many ... whose souls are wicked are dressed in handsome bodies, good stock, and wealth, and when the judgment takes place they have many witnesses appear to testify that they have lived just lives. Now the

---

35. All translations from the *Gorgias* are from Donald J. Zeyl.

judges are awestruck by these things and pass judgment at a time when they themselves are fully dressed, too, having put their eyes and ears and their whole bodies up as screens in front of their souls. All these things, their own clothing and that of those being judged, have proved to be obstructive to them. (523c–d)

The metaphor of being dressed and being naked proves particularly apt. When someone puts on clothing, the clothing becomes a partial screen between the naked body and others observing. Furthermore, clothing can serve to disguise by presenting to the world an appearance that does not faithfully indicate what lies beneath. Wolves may sneak in by wearing sheep's clothing. Ultimately, however, this hiding and disguising layer turns out to be extraneous decoration, dispensable in the end without fundamentally altering the body beneath.

This metaphor is helpful for our purposes because it encourages us to think carefully about those features of human beings that are only the outer layer—mere decoration or disguise—around the true self. Central to the myth is the idea that justice requires that judges base their judgments only on the features of the true self and not on these extraneous decorations. Having looked at the *Phaedo*, we may already guess that the body with its "eyes and ears" is mere clothing around the soul. This myth, however, adds more to our list of things that we may conventionally take to be the real person but that, upon inspection, turn out to be mere decoration. Zeus lists four things: (i) handsome bodies, (ii) good stock, (iii) wealth, and (iv) good reputation. We should pause for a moment to consider (ii)–(iv) because they point to a richer notion of the real self than a simple dichotomy between body and soul may suggest. All three of these items play a role in determining the social identity and status of the individual. An aristocrat in Athens may cherish his identity as a particular son of such and such august ancestors, who owns such and such fertile lands, and holds honor and respect with such and such powerful men. Conventionally, these items may exhaustively define *who one is*, the contents of one's social identity that establish one's value and station relative to others. Zeus, by contrast, requires that judges and judged discard all these things like an old garment, so that what lies *underneath* all this may serve as the basis of just judgment.

As we have already guessed, the true identity of the individual beneath the garment turns out to be the soul:

> They must be judged when they're stripped naked of all these things, for they should be judged when they're dead. The judge, too, should be naked, and dead, and with only his soul he should study only the soul of each person immediately upon his death (αὐτῇ τῇ ψυχῇ αὐτὴν τὴν ψυχὴν θεωροῦντα ἐξαίφνης ἀποθανόντος ἑκάστου), when he's isolated from all his kinsmen and has left behind on earth all that adornment, so that the judgment may be a just one. (523e)[36]

When the dead *individual* is stripped naked of all extraneous adornment, this means that only his *soul* is left.

Because both soul and body are substantial entities that can exist apart from one another after they separate, they also both continue to possess characteristics or "marks" (ἔνδηλα) after death (524b–c). For example, if a man earns floggings in life, the scars on the back of his corpse will continue to bear witness to this past for some time after death. Socrates twice divides the kinds of characteristics that remain on the body after death into two categories: those that the body possesses by nature (φύσει) and those that it acquires because of what happens to it (τροφῇ, 524b). This rather mundane description of corpses finds a more interesting mirror image in Socrates's description of souls:

> All that's in the soul is evident after it has been stripped naked of the body, both things that are natural to it and things that have happened to it, things that the person came to have in his soul as a result of his pursuit of each objective (τά τε τῆς φύσεως καὶ τὰ παθήματα ἃ διὰ τὴν ἐπιτήδευσιν ἑκάστου πράγματος ἔσχεν ἐν τῇ ψυχῇ ὁ ἄνθρωπος). (524d)

---

36. Compare the language we examined from the *Alcibiades* (130d) where Socrates says that in conversation, "one soul uses words to address another soul" (τῇ ψυχῇ πρὸς τὴν ψυχήν). For commentary on this connection see E. R. Dodds (Oxford, 1959) *ad loc.*

The just judgment of the naked individual, therefore, is based upon all that is evident in the soul after everything extraneous has been removed. These characteristics fall into two kinds: (i) things that are natural to the soul, and (ii) things that come to exist in the soul on the basis of the individual's actions. It seems, therefore, that we have an operative notion of the naked individual distinct from the ideal soul, qualitatively the same for everyone.[37] The naked individual carries the lasting consequences of his own actions and passions even after the covering of this life falls away, and these marks indicate both vices and virtues rather than negative corruptions only. Here, the marks of type (ii) do not always seem to be *alien* to the soul's own true nature but rather merely *added* to it.

On the basis of these two kinds of characteristic, the judges determine the fate of each individual and must be blind to all those extraneous details that only count as so much clothing. Socrates has a curious way, however, of expressing this blindness:

> So when they arrive before their judge—the people from Asia before Rhadamanthus—Rhadamanthus brings them to a halt and studies each person's soul without knowing whose it is (ὁ Ῥαδάμανθυς ἐκείνους ἐπιστήσας θεᾶται ἑκάστου τὴν ψυχήν, οὐκ εἰδὼς ὅτου ἐστίν). He's often gotten hold of the Great King, or some other king or potentate, and noticed that there's nothing sound in his soul but that it's been thoroughly whipped and covered with scars, the results of acts of perjury and of injustice, things that each of his actions has stamped upon his soul (ἃ ἑκάστη ἡ πρᾶξις αὐτοῦ ἐξωμόρξατο εἰς τὴν ψυχήν). (524d–525a)

Rhadamanthus does not know "who it is" that he has before him. This identity, this "who it is," corresponds to the individual being "the Great King" or "some other king or potentate," in other words, an identity of power or status in this life. A similar usage occurs on the next page:

---

37. Here again, we find another argument against the view of Sorabji that "Plato himself speaks as if all soul is one, indivisible except amongst bodies" (*Self*, 115). The souls in this myth, as in others, are clearly differentiated and distinct from one another on the basis of intrinsic features quite apart from embodiment.

So as I was saying, when Rhadamanthus the judge gets hold of someone [wicked] like that, he doesn't know a thing about him, neither who he is nor who his people are, except that he's somebody wicked (ἄλλο μὲν περὶ αὐτοῦ οὐκ οἶδεν οὐδέν, οὔθ᾽ ὅστις οὔθ᾽ ὧντινων, ὅτι δὲ πονηρός τις). (526b–c)

Here, Socrates pairs "who it is" with the a plural "whose" to which the individual belongs, apparently his family or tribe, that is, "his people." In other words, "who it is" expresses a social and conventional identity, everything expressed earlier by handsome bodies, good stock, wealth, and favorable testimony. In English, we may approximate this meaning of ὅστις by imagining an indignant celebrity that has been rudely served at the post office. We can imagine such a celebrity protesting, "Don't you know *who I am?*" This sense of identity stands in contrast to another sense of identity that the judge sees when the individual is stripped naked. Rhadamanthus sees only that the individual is "somebody wicked" (πονηρός τις). When the judge looks at the naked individual he sees the character of the soul taken by itself without trappings, a character established both by the nature of the soul and those events that make an impress upon it.

We have, therefore, an interesting notion of the true self. On the one hand, the real character of the naked individual does not include much of what people ordinarily take to be personal identity. Nearly all of what goes for one's "personality" or "identity" in ordinary discourse belongs to the "who it is" that Rhadamanthus is not allowed to see. On the other hand, the naked individual does retain individuating features that distinguish one soul from another. On the basis of these real distinctions between naked individuals, some travel down one road in the meadow of judgment and others down the other. It seems to me that this observation applies more generally to understanding the ideas of personhood and self throughout the dialogues. On the one hand, we should not read into the dialogues a post-Lockean conception of personal identity formed on the basis of social and idiosyncratic psychological factors like social relationships and continuity of episodic memory. Nor should we read into the dialogues anything like the personalist insistence on the absolute uniqueness of persons. On the other hand, we should not overreact against this contrast and deny that there is *any* operative notion of individual personhood or *any* distinctions between disembodied souls.

This points to another case where we do not find something in the dialogues but should be careful to avoid an overreaction: free will. The marks that stamp the soul are described in terms of both actions and passions (524b–d, 525a); both what I do and what is done to me potentially hold consequences for the character of my soul after death. This introduces the notion that—in at least some small part—the individual plays a role in shaping the character of soul that he will one day present to the judges. On the one hand, Zeus rules out judgments based on entirely extraneous factors, but, on the other hand, he also rules out judgments based on the given nature of the soul alone. This, of course, is a far cry from the claim that the individual's unconstrained free choices are the sole basis for his moral worth, but this should not cause us to overlook the rich picture of responsibility that does emerge from this and many other ancient texts.[38]

Republic

We will have much more to say about the theory of soul in the *Republic* when we turn, in the next chapter, to the theory of tripartition. Here, however, we will focus on the famous Myth of Er at the very end of the book. As in both the *Phaedo* and the *Gorgias*, Socrates follows the long argument of the *Republic* with a vivid description of our fate after death. He frames this description as the tale of a man named Er who comes back from the dead after ten days to tell what he has seen. As in the other myths, Socrates describes a judgment of souls for the lives they

---

38. See Michael Inwood, "Plato's Eschatological Myths," in *Plato's Myths*, ed. Catalin Partenie (Cambridge: Cambridge University Press, 2009), 44, for an enumeration of the ways that the freedom souls exhibit in the myths falls short of what he considers "genuinely free choice." See also Christopher Gill, *Personality in Greek Epic, Tragedy, and Philosophy*, 445–46, for a discussion of "radical" freedom, characteristic of modern theories, as opposed to the kind of freedom and responsibility we do see in ancient authors. For discussion of the absence of free will from both Plato and Aristotle see Michael Frede, *A Free Will*, 20.

have led, whether they have been just or unjust, and a corresponding allotment of fates. As in the *Phaedo*, Socrates describes a cyclical process of birth, death, and rebirth, with the possibility that an individual soul currently embodied in a human life may one day occupy a lower animal life instead (620a–d). The Myth of Er adds to the earlier myths, however, a greater emphasis on the individual's responsibility for the life chosen and hence for the soul's fate in judgment.

Er observes a gathering of souls choosing their upcoming lives just before another round of incarnation. The souls are presented with a large number of "models" or "patterns" (παραδείγματα) that depict various "lives" (βίοι, 617e–618b). The souls are given lots that establish the order in which they choose, but the large number of models affords good options even for the last soul (619b).

Next, a messenger comes to the souls on behalf of Lachesis to announce how all this will work:

> Ephemeral souls, this is the beginning of another cycle that will end in death. Your daemon or guardian spirit will not be assigned to you by lot (οὐχ ὑμᾶς δαίμων λήξεται); you will choose him (ἀλλ' ὑμεῖς δαίμονα αἱρήσεσθε). The one who has the first lot will be the first to choose a life to which he will then be bound by necessity (πρῶτος δ' ὁ λαχὼν πρῶτος αἱρείσθω βίον ᾧ συνέσται ἐξ ἀνάγκης). Virtue knows no master; each will possess it to a greater or less degree, depending on whether he values or disdains it. The responsibility lies with the one who makes the choice; the god has none (αἰτία ἑλομένου: θεὸς ἀναίτιος). (617d–e)

One motive for this complex arrangement seems to be the typically Greek sense that the stories of our lives follow an inevitable chain of cause and effect once started—as Oedipus illustrates all too painfully. Another motive that stands in tension with the first, however, seems to be Socrates' desire to remove from the gods all responsibility for our folly. If the course of my life is inevitable while I am in the middle of it but the gods did not dictate that I should live this way, then I must locate a root cause or explanation (αἰτία) outside the stream of events in this life. Within the myth itself this αἰτία lies with a primitive act of selection that one makes before one is born. Whether or not we (or Socrates for that matter) take this idea seriously as a literal event, understanding the myth requires that we at least imagine the individual soul who chooses as something logically distinct from the life that is chosen.

The notion of "life" (βίος) in play comes close to what we would call a "career" in English. It begins at birth, ends at death, and includes all those items that one puts on a *curriculum vitae*. Some of the models include "tyrannies," both those that last for the whole life and those that end "halfway through in poverty, exile, and beggary." Some models include fame on account of physical beauty, athletic prowess, or noble birth. Some models include wealth, poverty, sickness, or health. The choice of details here, especially the emphasis on tyranny as a kind of life, resembles closely the kinds of details that we called one's conventional identity in discussing the myth of the *Gorgias*, the "who it is" that Rhadamanthus is not allowed to see. Socrates tells us, however, that "the arrangement of the soul was not included in the model" (ψυχῆς δὲ τάξιν οὐκ ἐνεῖναι, 618b). The reason he cites is that the choice of model itself alters the arrangement (τάξις) of the soul doing the choosing. Apart, therefore, from the narrative details of an individual's life that constitute a "personality" or "career" we find a soul that is explanatorily prior to those details.

The effect of the choice upon the choosing soul's arrangement (τάξις) resembles closely the scars left upon the soul in the myth of the *Gorgias*. There we noticed a distinction between features of the soul that are inherent to the nature of the soul and features that an individual soul acquires because of both what it does and what is done to it. Here in the *Republic*, Socrates tells us that the wise man will know "all the things that are either naturally part of the soul or are acquired" (πάντα τὰ τοιαῦτα τῶν φύσει περὶ ψυχὴν ὄντων καὶ τῶν ἐπικτήτων, 618d). In both the *Gorgias* and *Republic*, the features that the soul acquires may be the marks of bad decisions, but they may also be the virtues gained by good ones, especially philosophical education. This yields a three-part rather than a two-part distinction. First we have the notion of the simple soul, that is, the soul *qua* soul, presumably identical for everyone. Second we add the idea of the individual soul insofar as it acquires a τάξις, for good or ill, according to its choices, actions, and passions. Third we have the idea of a purely embodied identity, complete with such things as good looks, noble birth, or political power. Notice again in this third category that the emphasis is not really on the body *per se* but on the shallowness of surface appearance and a conventional, social persona. Hence, the Socratic turn toward the soul is not primarily a turn away from materiality but a turn away from surface and convention.

Phaedrus

As with the *Republic*, we will have much more to say about the *Phaedrus* when it comes to the tripartite picture of the soul that we are given in the famous Charioteer Myth of the Palinode. For the purposes of this chapter, however, we can pull out just a few details from the myth that reveal much about the way Socrates is conceiving the relationship between soul and body. He begins:

> A soul that sheds its wings wanders until it lights on something solid, where it settles and takes on an earthly body, which then, owing to the power of this soul, seems to move itself (αὐτὸ αὑτὸ δοκοῦν κινεῖν διὰ τὴν ἐκείνης δύναμιν). The whole combination of soul and body is called a living thing (ζῷον τὸ σύμπαν ἐκλήθη, ψυχὴ καὶ σῶμα παγέν), or animal, and has the designation 'mortal' as well. Such a combination cannot be immortal, not on any reasonable account. In fact it is pure fiction, based neither on observation nor on adequate reasoning, that a god is an immortal living thing which has a body and a soul, and that these are bound together by nature for all time. (246c–d)

This confirms our analysis from the *Phaedo* (see chapter 2) that the biological organism (ζῷον), be it human, canine, or crab, is a composite of soul and body. This composite cannot be immortal precisely because things are liable to come apart at their joints (*Phaedo* 78c). The soul, by contrast, is the imperishable ἀρχή of motion within the organism so that the organic body *seems* to move itself. But if differences in biological species are determined by the nature of the compound rather than the soul that enters it, how are we to understand such terms as "human soul" or "divine soul" (245c)?

Quite simply, Socrates does *not* think that just any soul can enter just any compound. Because of the differences between the constitution of divine souls and human souls, the former are able to maintain their wings while the latter are prone to lose them (246a–b). When a soul does lose its wings, the divine law requires that its first incarnation (γένεσις) is not into the life of a wild beast (εἰς θήρειον φύσιν) but, rather, into one of nine kinds of human life (248d–e). If this life is lived well, such souls are raised by Justice to a place in heaven where they live in a manner worthy of "the life they led in human form" (ἀξίως οὗ ἐν ἀνθρώπου εἴδει ἐβίωσαν βίου, 249b). This talk of a temporary βίος in a "human form" reflects exactly the same usage of these terms in the *Phaedo* that we saw above. At the end of a cycle, the time comes for another incarnation:

> In the thousandth year both groups [that is, the just and the unjust] arrive at a choice and allotment of second lives (ἐπὶ κλήρωσίν τε καὶ αἵρεσιν τοῦ δευτέρου βίου), and each soul chooses the life it wants (αἱροῦνται ὃν ἂν θέλῃ ἑκάστη). From there, a human soul (ἀνθρωπίνη ψυχή) can enter a wild animal (εἰς θηρίου βίον), and a soul that was once human (ὅς ποτε ἄνθρωπος ἦν) can move from an animal (ἐκ θηρίου) to a human being again (πάλιν εἰς ἄνθρωπον). But a soul that never saw the truth cannot take a human shape (εἰς τόδε ἥξει τὸ σχῆμα), since a human being must understand speech in terms of general forms, proceeding to bring many perceptions together into a reasoned unity (δεῖ γὰρ ἄνθρωπον συνιέναι κατ' εἶδος λεγόμενον, ἐκ πολλῶν ἰὸν αἰσθήσεων εἰς ἓν λογισμῷ συναιρούμενον). That process is the recollection of the things our soul saw when it was traveling with god, when it disregarded the things we now call real and lifted up its head to what is truly real (εἰς τὸ ὂν ὄντως) instead. (249b–c)

> As I said, nature requires that the soul of every human being (πᾶσα ἀνθρώπου ψυχή) has seen reality (τὰ ὄντα); otherwise, no soul could have entered this sort of living thing (εἰς τόδε τὸ ζῷον). (249e–250a)

Throughout these passages we see a consistent terminology that corresponds with what we saw in the last chapter.

We may note again that as soon as Socrates mentions the recollection of forms he switches from generic language to the first-person plural: "That process is the recollection of the things *our* soul saw when it was traveling with god." This switch occurs again even more strongly on the next page:

> But beauty was radiant to see at that time when the souls, along with the glorious chorus (we were with Zeus, while others followed other gods), saw that blessed and spectacular vision and were ushered into the mystery that we may rightly call the most blessed of all. And *we* who celebrated it were wholly perfect and free of all the troubles that awaited us in time to come, and *we* gazed in rapture at sacred revealed objects that were perfect, and simple, and unshakable and blissful. That was the ultimate vision, and *we* saw it in pure light because *we were pure ourselves*, not buried in this thing *we are carrying around now*, which we call a body, locked in it like an oyster in its shell. (250b–c, emphasis added)

Again, we see that the present ability of Socrates to "bring many perceptions together into a reasoned unity" relies on an identity between this Socrates now and a soul that saw the forms then. This soul, being immortal, is not identical to the mortal compound of soul and body that it has entered into—the individual human being. Nevertheless, it makes sense to think of the class "our souls" as identical to the class of "human souls"—that is, those souls that *may* enter a human organism because they have at one time seen the forms, although they *may* also enter an animal organism or no organism at all (248c).

This begins to flesh out our picture of what "each one of us" means. "We" are a class of beings that contrasts, on the one hand, with the gods above and, on the other, with the purely brutal souls below. We are not gods because we cannot *guarantee* a stable apprehension of the forms, and we are not purely beasts because we all *have* apprehended the forms—if only in a momentary glance. We are not the sort of beings that are *necessarily* human because we can also sink to the level of animal life.

Indeed we aspire to a life that is more than merely human (250d). This yields a conception of the true Socrates as something that is not merely a soul *simpliciter* but, rather, a soul endowed with mind. What is more, it points to some kind of instability in that endowment. This instability will come to its clearest expression when we turn to the tripartition of the soul in the next chapter.

CHAPTER 3

Tripartition

LEAVING BEHIND THE BASIC DIVISION between the soul and the body, we will examine in this chapter the internal division of the soul itself. This shift in our discussion parallels a shift in the dialogues themselves—a shift that some scholars believe comes from a substantive change in Plato's views.[1] The *Phaedo* seems to present the soul as a simple entity while the *Republic* seems to present the soul as a complex of parts. Even for scholars that avoid an overly developmental reading of the dialogues, there seems to be at least a tension between these two pictures.[2] Fortunately, we need not immerse ourselves in this question for our present purposes. Socrates himself cautions his audience in the *Republic* that the tripartite account is not a "precise" account of the soul

---

1. David Bostock, *Plato's Phaedo*, 8, is representative of this view. He argues that the *Phaedo* understands the soul as a "single undivided unity," while the *Republic* understands it as a "compound of three parts." The latter view is, "clearly the more thoughtful of the two, and no one who had reached that view could return to the more naïve view of the *Phaedo* without considerable qualifications." Similarly, Hackforth, *Plato's Phaedo*, 11. T. M. Robinson, "Soul and Immortality in Republic x," *Phronesis* 12, no. 2 (1967): 147–51, at 148, argues that ψυχή in the *Phaedo* amounts to what becomes λογιστικόν in the *Republic*.

2. For examples of such scholars see Lloyd Gerson, "Platonic Dualism," *The Monist* 69, no. 3 (1986): 352–69, at 359, and McCabe, *Plato's Individuals*, 267. By the time he writes *Knowing Persons*, however, Gerson seems to soften the sharpness of this contrast. See *Knowing Persons*, 99.

(435c–d), and this should give us pause before we take it too dogmatically. Unfortunately—but conveniently for us—ancient thinkers seem to leave this caution unheeded, frequently attributing a straightforward theory of tripartition directly and unproblematically to Plato himself.[3] Insofar as we are looking for conceptual seeds in the dialogues that will later sprout into full-blown theories of the self, it is sufficient to notice that those passages examined in chapter 2 seem to primarily conceive of the self in terms of the soul *simpliciter* in contrast to the body while those passages that we will examine in this chapter add a further wrinkle because the structure of the soul itself appears to be complex.

This move immediately suggests the related question of whether anything within the total makeup of the soul counts as the *true* self rather than the whole soul. If we say that persons are a special kind of soul as opposed to all those non-persons that lack a noetic capacity, we may be tempted to simply identify the true self with the rational part of the soul. On this reading, the *Phaedo* teaches us that the true self is the soul rather than the whole human organism, and the *Republic* teaches us that the *really* true self is the rational *part* of the soul rather than the whole soul. As we will see, however, things are not quite so simple. In the first place, even in the *Republic* Socrates speaks occasionally of the whole soul in terms of the self. In the second place, part of the ethical point of tripartition is that one can choose to identify oneself more or less with any of the parts or with relative rankings of these parts, even if some of these identifications are less than ideal. This fluidity of identification suggests that the self is conceptually distinct from any of the three parts, even while *ideally* identified with the rational part. I will call this the "moving spotlight view" of the self, since which configuration of the three parts that is "lit up" as "me" depends on the direction I choose to point the "spotlight" of my conscious attention, affections, and motivations.

We saw in the last chapter that despite the potential pitfalls of "Platonic dualism," personalism owes a historical debt to this Platonic

---

3. For references and an interesting discussion of the way that division of the soul was received in antiquity see D. A. Rees, "Bipartition of the Soul in the Early Academy," *The Journal of Hellenic Studies* 77, no. 1 (1957): 112–18.

division between body and soul, because it is precisely within the Platonic tradition that an emphasis on the transcendence and spiritual interiority of the person—the original purpose of the dualism—finds its home and its most consistent defense against the rival traditions of reductionistic and mechanistic thinking. In this chapter, we will go even further. We will identify three core personalist themes as flowing directly from the tripartite account of the soul: (i) the personalist conception of freedom and self-mastery, (ii) the conception of personal identity as an achievement, and (iii) the path of self-knowledge, conceived as the investigation of the interior workings of the soul, as the path to this free personal identity.

Just as the division between body and soul was not introduced for its own sake but as a way to motivate the turn away from conventional shallowness toward the spiritual and eternal, so too the tripartite division within the soul is not introduced for its own sake but as a way to motivate a particular conception of *freedom*. According to this conception, we should identify ourselves with one aspect of our psychology, our νοῦς, over and against other aspects of our psychology, our appetites, our instincts, our concern for honor and appearances, and so on. Freedom, on this view, is the liberation of the higher, nobler side of ourselves from the lower, chaotic side. We achieve this through a progressive spiritual quest both of self-knowledge (discovering more and more that the higher side is who we really are) and self-mastery (learning practically how to act from our higher side as our principal, but not exclusive, source of motivation).

As with our discussion of the dualism, the way that Plato achieves these personalist desiderata is not without its shortcomings. The later tradition has exposed potentially grave misunderstandings or important lacunae, but that is the wonderful thing about a tradition: It allows us to extend and correct the ideas of our forebears, without whom we would not be smart enough to do any extending and correcting.

One terminological note before we begin: Throughout I will frequently use the traditional terminology referring to the highest part of the soul as the "rational part" of the soul. Both words in this formulation, however, are potentially misleading. First, "rational" should be taken not in the sense of a cold discursive rationalism, but ultimately as referring to a non-discursive νοῦς animated by a yearning for truth. Nothing here should be taken to imply "head versus heart." Second, Plato never uses the word "part" when referring to the three "parts" of the soul. In Greek, the names of these "parts" are typically just substantive adjectives or participles—"the thinking," "the desiring," "the honor-loving"—and sometimes simple substantives—λόγος, νοῦς, θυμός.

Self-Control

Shortly before he launches into his famous argument for the tripartition of the soul in book 4 of the *Republic*, Socrates conspicuously notes how odd it is to talk about self-control:

> Isn't the expression "self-control" (κρείττω αὑτοῦ) ridiculous? The stronger self that does the controlling is the same as the weaker self that gets controlled (ὁ γὰρ ἑαυτοῦ κρείττων καὶ ἥττων δήπου ἂν αὑτοῦ εἴη καὶ ὁ ἥττων κρείττων), so that only one person is referred to in all such expressions (ὁ αὐτὸς γὰρ ἐν ἅπασιν τούτοις προσαγορεύεται). (430e–431a)

On the surface, Socrates' complaint seems to be against the strangeness of a Greek phrase, but the problem is more than linguistic. We cannot differentiate a completely simple or singular entity according to aspects or parts. Hence, if we attribute contradictory properties to such an entity, in this case *controlling* (that is, being stronger, κρείττων) and *being controlled* (that is, being weaker, ἥττων), we have a real and metaphysically problematic contradiction. Somehow we must split up the entity in question.

Interestingly, Socrates does not frame this as a conflict between soul and body or between soul and "human being" as we may have anticipated from the material in the last chapter. Instead, he focuses on the soul alone:

The expression is apparently trying to indicate that, in the soul (περὶ τὴν ψυχήν) of that very person (ἐν αὐτῷ τῷ ἀνθρώπῳ), there is a better part (τὸ μὲν βέλτιον) and a worse one (τὸ δὲ χεῖρον) and that, whenever the naturally better part (τὸ βέλτιον φύσει) is in control of the worse, this is expressed by saying that the person is self-controlled or master of himself. (431a)

According to this way of glossing the phrase, one part or aspect of the soul is strong and in control, while another is weak and in submission.

We see a very similar argument in both the *Gorgias* and the *Laws*. In the *Gorgias*, Socrates explains that what the "many" mean by the phrase "rules himself" (ἑαυτοῦ ἄρχων) is "being self-controlled and master of oneself, ruling the pleasure and appetites within oneself" (491d–e). The latter phrase is a gloss upon the first. In other words, the "oneself" in the phrase "master of oneself" is not really *oneself*, strictly speaking but, rather, "the pleasure and appetites *within* oneself."

Again, we find the Athenian Stranger taking a very similar line in the *Laws*. He asks Clinias the puzzling question whether a man should "think of *himself* as his own enemy." Clinias answers that indeed the "first and best of victories" is the one that a man wins over himself and that "this way of speaking points to a war against ourselves within each one of us."[4] Like Socrates in *Republic* 4, the Stranger points out a similar logical puzzle in this way of speaking: "You hold that each one of us is either 'conqueror of' or 'conquered by' himself" (εἷς ἕκαστος ἡμῶν ὁ μὲν κρείττων αὑτοῦ, ὁ δὲ ἥττων ἐστί, 626d–627a). Here the stranger simply replaces Socrates' ὁ αὐτός with εἷς ἕκαστος ἡμῶν. If we treat each person as purely one (notice the emphatic place and use of εἷς), it makes no sense to ascribe such opposite properties as *conqueror of* and *conquered by* in relation to the same thing. The Stranger does not actually solve this puzzle in the case of the individual but rather makes use of cities and households. We can say that a city overcomes itself when the class of virtuous citizens wins out over the class of vicious citizens and conversely that it is weaker than itself when the situation is reversed. The implication is that an individual

---

4. Notice the way that Clinias naturally slides into using ἡμῶν ἕκαστος when he begins to conceive of an abstract notion of the self within which a war is taking place: ταῦτα γὰρ ὡς πολέμου ἐν ἑκάστοις ἡμῶν ὄντος.

is "stronger than himself" when the better "population" within his constitution gains mastery over the worse. Much later, he identifies anger as "one of the constituent elements" in the soul and defines injustice as "the mastery of the soul by anger, fear, pleasure, pain, envy and desires, whether they lead to any actual damage or not" (863b, 863e–864a). Although this is not exactly the tripartite account of the *Republic*, we have the idea that there is conflict *within the soul* together with the idea that the question of which element will gain the upper hand is of the utmost ethical importance.

If Socrates, then, is "stronger than himself," what does this make Socrates? Is *Socrates himself* strong or weak? Two plausible interpretations come immediately to mind: (i) Socrates himself is the whole soul. The phrase, "only one person [lit. 'the same,' ὁ αὐτός] is referred to in all such expressions" seems to favor this interpretation. Just as a single top as a whole can both stand still and move at the same time in virtue of its stationary axis and spinning circumference (436d–e), so too Socrates himself is both master and mastered in virtue of one element within him that does the mastering and another that is mastered. (ii) Socrates himself is only the part that gains mastery. Self-mastery is a position of victory and strength *for Socrates* only if Socrates himself is identified with the better part of the soul (τὸ βέλτιον). If this were not so, the virtue of moderation would be a mixed blessing *for Socrates* as it would require that *he* is both winner and loser—part of him wins, but the part of him that loses has just as much claim to being him. Instead, the overall tenor of the passage suggests that gaining self-mastery would be altogether good for its possessor and this requires that the aspect of the soul that loses be somehow alienated from the identity of the self-controlled person.[5]

---

5. Rachana Kamtekar, "Speaking with the Same Voice as Reason: Personification in Plato's Psychology," in *Plato and the Divided Self*, ed. Rachel Barney, Tad Brennan, and Charles Brittain (Cambridge University Press, 2012), 77–101 94, points out that insofar as "self-control" is a term of praise we implicitly identify the self with that which controls rather than that which is controlled. She also argues, however, that Socrates wishes to preserve the insight contained in the phrase that what we seek to control is not wholly exterior to ourselves either. Gerson, *Knowing Persons* 106, mentions how natural it is to speak of being "overcome" by one's anger or emotions but how unnatural it is to speak of being "overcome" by one's rational decision, even if it is a mistaken decision. He further argues that this is so because we can easily distinguish between a person and his emotions but we cannot so easily distinguish between a person and his mind.

Explaining Internal Conflict

As we enter Socrates's argument for tripartition proper, a puzzle related to the self immediately comes to the surface. Socrates makes his argument on the basis of motivational conflict, and he resolves this by referring the contrary motivations to distinct parts or aspects of the soul in a manner similar to his solution to the problem of self-mastery above. The puzzle is this: the problem of motivational conflict only arises if we treat these motivations as taking place within a single self, and yet Socrates sometimes speaks of the distinct elements within the soul as though they were each distinct selves, complete with cognition, desires, and agency.[6] Just how many selves are there in this picture, and is there any one self that has a rightful claim to actually being Socrates?[7]

Socrates begins his argument for tripartition by separating the rational part from the appetitive part. He does this by appealing to the example of "thirsty people who don't wish to drink" (439c). In such cases, Socrates says that we cannot refer the contrary predicates *wishes to drink*

---

[6]. As just one indication of how strongly this latter perspective appeals to contemporary interpreters of Plato, Barney, Brennan, and Brittain are able to speak, in the introduction to their recent collection of papers on tripartition, of the "growing consensus" that the parts of the soul in the *Republic* are "robustly agent-like individuals," 2–3. Terence Irwin, *Plato's Ethics* (Oxford University Press, 1995) 217, states that Plato "conceives the parts of the soul as analogous to agents." Central to his account of the development of Plato's ethics, Christopher Bobonich, *Plato's Utopia Recast: His Later Ethics and Politics* (Oxford University Press, 2002) 217, argues that Plato is committed in the middle-period dialogues to a "partitioning thesis" according to which "individual human beings consist of distinct agent-like parts." According to Bobonich, the *Phaedo* treats the soul and body as two distinct agent-like parts that make up the human being, while the *Republic* refines this account to recognize three distinct agent-like parts internal to the soul itself, downgrading the role of the body. By "agent-like" Bobonich means that "each is treated as the ultimate subject of psychological affections, activities, and capacities that are normally attributed to the person as a whole," 219. This partitioning thesis, however, is one that Bobonich thinks Plato ultimately gives up by the time he writes the *Laws*. Kamtekar, "Speaking with the Same Voice as Reason" 79, argues that "Plato's psychology represents our motivations as themselves person-like ('personifies' our motivations) with the aim of showing us the lineaments of philosophic virtue and of the self-transformation required for its development."

[7]. For an excellent statement of the problem here see Gerson, *Knowing Persons*, 105: "If we insist on literal division [of the soul], are we not led to a view of a nominal soul or person that is really three souls or three selves? Are we not led, as the predictable and just complaint has it, to the positing of homunculi, a little appetitive man, a little spirited man, and a little rational man, a sort of committee where each member is vying for dominance?" See also Bobonich, *Plato's Utopia Recast* 248–254, for an admirably thorough analysis of the regress problem that this picture involves.

and *refuses to drink* to a perfectly simple entity, but rather must refer them to different parts within these people:

> Isn't it that there is something in their soul, bidding them to drink, and something different, forbidding them to do so, that overrules the thing that bids. (439c)

The language of "bidding" and "forbidding" seems to personify the parts within the soul, as though the part that bids were a thirsty self asking the whole human being to take the drink and the part that forbids were a more cautious self that asks the whole human being to refrain. I will call this way of conceiving the three parts of the soul as three little complete selves within the person the "homunculi" interpretation.[8]

Socrates frequently uses language throughout the *Republic* that seems to favor this interpretation. As just one example, he says that the virtue of moderation occurs when the three parts "agree" with one another that "the calculating part ought to rule" so that they "don't raise faction against it" (442c–d). On the one hand, we can surely dismiss some of Socrates's talk as mere colorful metaphor, reinforcing the link that Socrates wishes to draw between justice in the soul and justice in the city. The soul is like a city with little citizens running around inside it. In order to deflate the significance of this picture, we might attempt to scrub away all personifying talk from Socrates's characterization of tripartition. Even once we have accounted for colorful metaphor, however, we are left with substantive difficulties. For example, Socrates says that a person is courageous when

> his spirited part preserves, through pains and pleasures, what has been proclaimed by the speeches (τὸ ὑπὸ τῶν λόγων παραγγελθὲν) about that which is terrible and that which is not. (442c)

---

8. In this terminology I am following Gerson, *Knowing Persons*, 100–24, who argues against this view, claiming instead that "a 'part' of the soul is just an ἀρχή of action." Compare Jennifer Whiting, "Psychic Contingency in the *Republic*," in *Plato and the Divided Self*, 174–208, at 178, who makes a distinction between "realist" interpretations of the *Republic* that read the parts as robustly agent-like and "deflationist" interpretations that read all this as mere metaphor. Julia Annas, *An Introduction to Plato's Republic* (Oxford: Oxford University Press, 1981), 142, refers to the regress problem that this interpretation sets up as the "Homunculus Problem."

Perhaps we can dismiss "proclaim" as a metaphor, but we may still wonder how the spirited part can do anything remotely like what Socrates describes if we do not conceive of it at all in terms appropriate to a complete conscious agent.[9] Similar problems come up again in book 10 when Socrates mentions that each of the three parts of the soul have their own distinct pleasures and their own distinct desires (580d). A little further, he mentions that "the part of the soul that forms belief contrary to the measurements couldn't be the same as the part that believes in accord with them" (603a). If all cognition belongs to the rational part, how can there be any beliefs at all going on apart from it?[10] With the parts characterized in this way, the conflict between them seems very much like the conflict that occurs between different persons with different beliefs, agendas, and preferences.

So far, I have attempted to resist an all-too-easy escape from the homunculi interpretation that would simply dismiss Socrates' talk as metaphor and read the three parts as unproblematic faculties or aspects within a single self. Nevertheless, we *do* need to escape from the homunculi interpretation because it too is untenable. While many objections have been offered against it in the literature,[11] I want to focus on one in particular because of our special interest in identifying the self. The kind of conflict that generates Socrates' argument for tripartition in the first place makes sense only if we view it as a conflict within a single self.[12] To

---

9. For the particular issues involved with attributing cognitive ability to the non-rational parts, see Irwin, *Plato's Ethics*, 218: "If [Plato] treats the two non-rational parts of the soul as though they were capable of behaving like reasonable people, he seems to be treating each part as though it were an agent with its own rational part. To understand how this 'agent' makes its choices, we must presumably divide its soul into three; if we must also make each of these three parts an agent, we seem to be forced into a vicious regress."

10. For an admirably cautious exposition of the issues here see James Wilberding, "Curbing One's Appetites in Plato's *Republic*," in *Plato and the Divided Self*, 128–49, at 132, who argues that the lower parts of the soul possess modes of "cognition," even "conceptualization," that fall short of a full-blown ability to "reason."

11. The foremost objections seem to be those stemming from the threat of regress (see above) and those stemming from the unity of consciousness. On the latter point see Bobonich, *Plato's Utopia Recast*, 254: "The *Republic*'s partitioning theory commits Plato to denying the unity of the person. Specifically, it commits him to denying that there is a single ultimate subject of all of a person's psychic states and activities. What seems to be a single psychic entity is in fact a composite of three distinct and durable subjects."

12. Annas, *An Introduction to Plato's Republic*, 142, notices this.

see this point more vividly, let us imagine contrary motivational predicates belonging to two distinct selves, Philo and Dion. Philo wishes to drink, while Dion refuses to drink. We do not generate a metaphysical puzzle here. Philo wishes to drink, so he does. Dion refuses to drink, so he does not. The conflict in Socrates' initial example, however, comes from desire and repugnance vying to determine the single action of a single self. We might imagine Philo and Dion coming into conflict because they cannot both satisfy their wishes. They are escaped prisoners chained together, say, and Philo wishes to flee north, while Dion wishes to flee south. They may settle this conflict in any number of ways, by persuasion or trickery or violence, but any resolution will involve two distinct agents committing two distinct acts more or less in parallel. The kind of conflict that Socrates appeals to, however, arises within a single agent over what that agent is going to do—ultimately who that agent is going to be.

As further support for this line of thinking, we find several passages in the *Republic* where Socrates refers to the person as a whole interacting with or organizing all three parts.[13] We find a prime example of this way of speaking in book 4:[14]

> [Justice] isn't concerned with someone's doing his own externally, but with what is inside him, with what is truly himself and his own. One who is just does not allow any part of himself to do the work of another part or allow the various classes within him to meddle with each other. He regulates well what is really his own and rules himself. He puts himself in order, is his own friend, and harmonizes the three parts of himself like three limiting notes in a musical scale—high, low, and middle. He binds together those parts and any others there may be in between, and from having been many things he becomes entirely one, moderate and harmonious. (443c–d)

We can identify several possible interpretations of the "he" in this passage. First, Socrates could intend "he" to refer to a fourth part of the soul that governs or manages the others. On this reading, we have

---

13. This is noticed by Gerson, *Knowing Persons*, 112.
14. Another convenient example would be book 9, 571d–572a.

a mysterious *ego* somehow distinct from and set over the three parts. Second, Socrates could intend "he" to refer to the whole soul over and above the three parts. On this reading, the self would be identical to the soul *simpliciter*. Third, Socrates could intend "he" to refer to the rational part alone (or, what is much less likely, the spirited part or the appetitive part alone) in its capacity as manager. On this reading, the rational part is identified with the agent when it is conceived as doing the managing and referred to as one of the agent's parts when it is conceived as being managed along with the other parts. Fourth, Socrates could intend "he" to refer indefinitely to *whatever* part or arrangement of parts actually prevails in determining what the person does.

I find this last interpretation superior to the first three because it makes sense of how each of the parts can be personified without resorting to the homunculi interpretation. If Socrates consistently identifies the agent himself with something other than, say, the appetitive part, then we should expect to see the appetitive part characterized throughout as merely a subpersonal force alien to the agent. As it stands, however, we *sometimes* see the appetitive part characterized in this way, but *sometimes* see it characterized as though it were *a version of the agent himself*. I suggest that this is because the "he" is something of a moving spotlight, picking out whatever source of motivation or relative hierarchy of motivational sources actually determines what an agent does in any given situation. This also makes sense of why Socrates speaks of the "he" arranging all three parts rather than simply speaking of the rational part arranging the other two parts beneath itself. Finally, I think this last interpretation is our best candidate for making sense of the passages we will examine in the next sections that seem to identify the true self with the rational part *in ideal cases*.

This way of understanding the identity of the agent as something up for grabs can also help us make sense of an otherwise difficult passage. In attempting to distinguish spirit from appetite, Socrates appeals to the story of Leontius:

> Leontius, the son of Aglaion, was going up from the Piraeus along the outside of the North Wall when he saw some corpses lying at the executioner's feet. He had an appetite to look at them (ἅμα μὲν ἰδεῖν ἐπιθυμοῖ) but at the same time he was disgusted and turned away (ἅμα δὲ αὖ δυσχεραίνοι καὶ ἀποτρέποι ἑαυτόν). For a time he struggled with himself and covered his face, but, finally, overpowered by the appetite, he pushed his eyes wide open and rushed towards the corpses, saying, "Look for yourselves, you evil wretches, take your fill of the beautiful sight!" (439e–440a)

In this story, Leontius's anger is aroused against *his own* behavior. It may well be that he would become indignant at another person looking upon corpses, but that kind of righteous indignation is not the emotion that Socrates here describes. Furthermore, we may find it at least a little strange that Socrates fails to describe any of Leontius's peers looking on in a situation where Leontius's honor-loving part is supposed to become aroused. Alongside anger at what others are doing and anger at what others think of me, however, I can also become angry over what I myself have done contrary to my own best intentions or sense of what is honorable. Leontius becomes frustrated because he himself (as the subject of appetite) does the very thing that he himself (as the subject of honor and shame) struggled to avoid. We should notice especially that in his frustration Leontius addresses his own eyes as though they were other persons and attributes the action to them, doing anything he can to distance himself from himself.

Rather than characterize the struggle between reason and appetite in this story as a struggle between two complete selves, on the one hand, or two subpersonal psychological faculties, on the other, we might instead characterize it as a struggle between two distinct versions of Leontius battling over who Leontius himself will be. On the one hand, we also have Leontius as the subject of appetites. This version of Leontius finds himself wanting to look. On the other hand, we have Leontius as the subject of honor and shame. This version of Leontius finds himself wanting to look away. One source of action within Leontius drives him to be the kind of person who looks at corpses and enjoys it. Another source of action within him drives him to be the kind of person that finds such things disgusting. These elements within his psyche cannot both succeed because they are fighting to determine a single identity.[15] This helps to explain why his sense of honor would become engaged to the point of frustration. The action of looking at corpses says something about who he is.[16] If I am right in this interpretation, then we can find no simple way to say which of the three parts of the soul *is* Leontius himself, for everything hinges on which of the three sources of action carries the day.[17]

In order to understand the fluid nature of Leontius's identity, I find Lloyd Gerson's notion of "identifying with" a soul-part to be helpful:

> The endowed person [in contrast with the ideal or achieved person], I suggest, "identifies" with one or another parts of his soul in much the way we would say that someone identified with a cause or an institution or another person. This identification is equivalent to endorsing the rule of either the rational, or the spirited, or the appetitive part of the soul.[18]

---

15. Similarly Gerson, *Knowing Persons*, 109: "When Leontius thinks 'Should I or should I not?' he is neither quarrelling with an appetite nor figuring out what he ought to do. He already *knows* what he ought to do. The quarrel is rather between Leontius as a subject of the appetite and Leontius as a subject of rational thought."

16. See the analysis of spirit in this passage as essentially involving reference to the self and to an ideal with which one wants to identify the self in Annas, *An Introduction to Plato's Republic*, 128: "[Leontius] did not want to be the *kind of person* capable of doing such a thing." Kamtekar, "Speaking with the Same Voice as Reason," 88: "Assigning motivations to distinct and evaluatively loaded *personae* facilitates disowning some of one's motivations and identifying with others."

17. Compare this to the "principle of psychological hegemony" in Eric Brown, "The Unity of the Soul in Plato's *Republic*," in *Plato and the Divided Self*, 53–73, at 68–69. According to this principle, "different kinds of people are ruled by different soul-parts," where "to be ruled by a soul-part is to take the ends of that soul-part to be one's ends." Brown claims that this principle emerges as the best explanation of the various things Socrates says throughout books 8 and 9 about different kinds of people and their psychology. We find a similar principle in Gerson, *Knowing Persons*, 115–16. Another scholar who endorses this principle, but argues that it is partition alone that does the theoretical work here rather than the personification of the parts, is Kamtekar, "Speaking with the Same Voice as Reason," 83. While I agree that personifying the parts is not strictly necessary to establish the principle of psychological hegemony, the conceit does help to imaginatively portray different possible versions of the self. In other words, I can more easily imagine what I would be like should I align myself wholly with the spirited part if I imagine the spirited part as a little version of me complete with thoughts, desires, and goals. We can observe a similar move at work in popular films where the traditional angel and demon on opposite shoulders of a character have the face of the character himself and magnified elements of his own personality (for example, *The Emperor's New Groove*).

18. Gerson, *Knowing Persons*, 117.

This notion, says Gerson, helps to explain why we find some passages (for example, *Republic* 4.443c–d, discussed above) that seem to speak of an agent over and above the parts organizing them or yielding to them, while we also find passages that seem to identify the rational part as the real underlying agent:

> If we try to characterize the agent involved in identification, it is difficult to do so in terms other than those that would be applied to the characterization of the rational part of the soul. That is, if we imagine a person "turning over" government in his soul to the spirited part in such a way as to fix his character, we must imagine reflective consideration on his part. Plato does exactly this.[19]

No doubt, Leontius *ought* to be the sort of person who consistently aligns his actions with his reasonable thinking. That is to say, Leontius himself *ought* to be identical with Leontius the subject of rational thought. This gives us some grounds for saying that the "real" or the "true" Leontius is the rational part of his soul, but perhaps it would be better to call this the "ideal" Leontius. Unfortunately, who Leontius actually is falls short of who Leontius himself aspires to be and who he shows himself to be by his own cognitive activity even while abandoning himself to his appetites—hence the frustration. We can say, then, that the "true self" is the rational part of the soul only in the sense that ideally *who we are* would be just the same as *who we know we should be*. As a matter of experience, however, we find ourselves frequently separated from this ideal, requiring education and struggle if we are to achieve our own truest and best identity.

The Human Being Within

Socrates closes book 9 of the *Republic* with the famous image of the soul as a human, a lion, and a many-headed beast (588c–592a). He introduces this image in order to "return to the first things we said" about whether "injustice profits a completely unjust person who is believed to

19. Ibid.

be just" (588b). He does this by painting with words the kind of image "in which many different kinds of things are said to have grown together naturally into one" such as the Chimera or Cerberus (588c). We should notice these framing comments because they establish two points that one may easily overlook about the image. First, we must interpret this image as an attempt by Socrates to portray the desirability of justice. Second, the image involves the tension between inherently different kinds of thing that have been naturally united into a single organism. In ordinary life, we see lions as a single kind of thing and human beings as a single kind of thing—two distinct natures. In myth, however, we may join these two natures that are alien to one another into a single composite nature by describing, for example, a lion with the head of a man. By his image, Socrates suggests that what we ordinarily take to be the simple nature of a human being includes a psychology composed of diverse and perhaps opposed elements that are nevertheless bound together "by nature" into a single kind of thing. This should provoke us to wonder what sort of thing we ourselves are. After describing the three creatures within the soul, Socrates tells Glaucon to "join the three of them into one, so that they somehow grow together naturally" (588d). The "somehow" here suggests that we should find the union surprising, and indeed the image *is* rather hard to picture.

Because he describes the rational part of the soul as a human being (ἄνθρωπος) we may suppose that Socrates means to emphasize a special connection between this part and the whole human organism. Socrates confirms this emphasis when he describes the covering that surrounds the three inner creatures:

> Fashion around [the three inner creatures] the image of one of them, that of a human being (ἄνθρωπος) so that anyone who sees only the outer covering and not what's inside will think it is a single creature, a human being (ἄνθρωπος). (588d–e)

Two interpretations are readily available: (i) Socrates describes the rational part as a human being because he wants us to understand that this element is what makes us human, that it is the most human aspect of our psychology, and that the other aspects are subhuman.[20] (ii) Socrates describes the rational part as a human being because he wants to say that this is the true self. In place of the exterior, conventional identity of a person, he wants to identify the rational part of the soul as the "inner person."[21] These two interpretations are not exclusive. It may be that we should identify the rational part as the true self *because* it is what makes us human in contrast to the merely animal elements within us.

In favor of interpretation (i), Socrates says that "[f]ine things are those that subordinate the beastlike parts (τὰ θηριώδη) of our nature to the human (ὑπὸ τῷ ἀνθρώπῳ)—or better, perhaps, to the divine (ὑπὸ τῷ θείῳ)" (589c–d). We must delay until the next chapter our discussion of the tantalizing possibility that something within us is not just human but superhuman. For now, however, we can see that Socrates exploits his depiction of the rational part as a human being to make the subordination of the other two parts seem more appealing than the reverse. On the whole, things are better off for all the parts and the whole human organism when the human element within rules over the animal elements rather than letting the animal elements run wild (588e–589d). The idea seems to be that in ordinary life we see the relationship between humans and domesticated animals often benefiting both the humans and the animals. When we observe situations where wild animals gain control of human beings, however, this invariably profits the animals at the expense of the human beings. This happens, in part, because human beings are able to calculate rationally about how to cultivate animals, and this suggests a natural relationship of superiority.

Already we see one way that the image makes justice desirable, but

---

20. See Sabina Lovibond, "Plato's Theory of Mind," 48, for this view.

21. See Richard Sorabji, *Self*, 116: "It is because the reason is described as the man or human that Plato is taken to mean that reason is the true man or the true self." A related but not quite identical line of interpretation comes from Annas, *An Introduction to Plato's Republic*, 145: "The image unfortunately makes clear that while desire and spirit do not reproduce the characteristics of the whole person, reason seems to." Annas qualifies this "seems" by noting that the interests and aims of the inner human and the whole human coincide only in the ideal case of the just person. I would point out that Socrates explicitly describes the whole human animal as the copy of the inner original rather than the other way around as Annas's complaint would have it. Gerson, *Knowing Persons*, 125–30, straightforwardly interprets the "human being within the human" as a reference to the true self.

we should also notice a second way that Socrates subtly uses this image to make his appeal. Because we are humans we naturally picture ourselves within the image as being the little inner human rather than one of the animals. We intuitively think of the situation in which the many-headed beast rips the little human apart as terrible for us because we imagine ourselves being ripped apart rather than ourselves enjoying a tasty meal. This identification, then, of the lower two parts of the soul with animals lends itself toward alienating those elements of our psychology. One can easily think of someone saying, "It isn't really *me* that feels this sexual urge; it's merely the evolutionary hold-over of animal instincts within me." Someone who thinks this way tacitly supposes that he himself must be identified with the aspect of his psychology that rises above the merely animal sphere, and part of the appeal in Socrates's image relies on this kind of supposition.

In favor of interpretation (ii), Socrates subtly shifts from speaking about the rational part as though it were an element *within* the just person to speaking as though the inner human being were the just person himself:

> Wouldn't someone who maintains that just things are profitable be saying, first, that all our words and deeds should ensure that the human being within this human being (τοῦ ἀνθρώπου ὁ ἐντὸς ἄνθρωπος) has the most control; second, that he should take care of the many-headed beast as a farmer does his animals, feeding and domesticating the gentle heads and preventing the savage ones from growing; and, third, that he should make the lion's nature his ally, care for the community of all his parts, and bring them up in such a way that they will be friends with each other and with himself? (589a–b)

In the first description of the just person, we have a clear distinction between "the human being within" and "this human being." In the second and third descriptions, however, it becomes difficult to say who the farmer is. On the one hand, Socrates says "his parts" so that we should naturally read the "he" throughout as the whole just person, but, on the other hand, the image lends itself to picturing the inner human being as the farmer tending the lion and the many-headed beast. The phrase "he should make the lion's nature his ally" especially suggests that we should think of the farmer as the rational part since elsewhere Socrates has spoken of the "alliance" that the spirited part makes with the rational part (for example, 440b). It may be difficult to settle definitively whether the farmer in the metaphor is the rational part or the whole person because Socrates himself thinks of the rational part (in the just person at any rate) as a representative of the person as a whole, just as he conceives the ruling class within the just city as representative of the city as a whole.[22]

As we saw in our discussion of Leontius, there may be a separation between the ideal and the actual identity of the self. For this reason, I think that Richard Sorabji's flat identification of the inner human being as the true self is too simplistic. Instead, the image suggests that the rational part is that aspect of our psychology that we *should* identify with because doing so leads to the best state of affairs for us. Further, when we truly live up to what it means to be human we *do* identify with it because the rational part is what makes us human. In point of fact, however, many live bestial lives, identifying themselves instead with those aspects of their psychology that do not represent their own real interests.

What Kind of Thing Am I?

Before we turn to examine the famous image from the *Phaedrus* that also includes an inner human being, we must pause to examine an important passage from early in the *Phaedrus* that will frame what comes later. Before launching into his famous speeches, Socrates explains why he does not practice, like other "intellectuals," the rational demythologization of traditional stories:

> But I have no time for such things; and the reason, my friend, is this. I am still unable, as the Delphic inscription orders, to know myself (γνῶναι

---

22. See Lovibond, "Plato's Theory of Mind," 50, for a similar idea in her discussion of what she calls the "world-historic" idea within Plato of the centered or integrated subject where "every constituent of our subjectivity should be supervised and, as far as possible, controlled ... by a central agency which is representative of the self as a whole."

ἐμαυτόν); and it really seems to me ridiculous to look into other things before I have understood that. This is why I do not concern myself with them. I accept what is generally believed, and, as I was just saying, I look not into them but into my own self (σκοπῶ οὐ ταῦτα ἀλλ᾽ ἐμαυτόν): Am I a beast (τι θηρίον) more complicated and savage (πολυπλοκώτερον καὶ μᾶλλον ἐπιτεθυμμένον) than Typhon, or am I a tamer, simpler (ἡμερώτερόν τε καὶ ἁπλούστερον) animal (ζῷον) with a share in a divine and gentle nature (θείας τινὸς καὶ ἀτύφου μοίρας φύσει μετέχον)? (229e–230a)

We should notice right away that Socrates does not interpret the Delphic inscription as an injunction to know himself as an individual in contrast to other persons, to "find himself" in the contemporary therapeutic sense of finding his special identity. Rather, he interprets it as an injunction to investigate what *sort* of being he is, what *nature* he has a share in.[23] In this investigation, he offers a contrast consisting of three pairs of opposing terms: (i) "complex" versus "simple," (ii) "savage" versus "tamer" and "gentle," and (iii) "beast" versus "divine." Like the metaphor of the inner beast in the *Republic*, the complicated points toward the subhuman and wild because it suggests internal disharmony and even outright conflict. As we will see below in the myth of Glaucon, simplicity points toward the superhuman because it suggests internal unity, freedom from conflict, and purity. While we must postpone our discussion of divinity until the next chapter, we may notice that Socrates allows both the possibility of a bestial self and the possibility of a divine self. Being human seems to mean that both are possible answers to the question, "What am I?" Although we may suspect him of irony in his declaration of ignorance, we should take seriously the idea that Socrates is "still unable" to know the answer to this question. Perhaps Socrates allows these various possibilities and invites us to join his perplexity because the answer to this question depends on the course of life we adopt.

We find a further caution when we come to the image of the soul as a

23. On this point I disagree with Gerson, *Knowing Persons*, 145–46, who holds that "self-knowledge in the dialogues is something more than the knowledge of the kind of thing a soul is. It is the first-person knowledge of my personhood." As far as I can find in the dialogues, references to self-knowledge can best be understood as knowledge of the kind of thing one is and what this means for how one should live, as Socrates makes explicit here.

chariot because Socrates explicitly states that he is not going to describe "what the soul actually is" (οἶον μέν ἐστι) because such a description would "require a very long account" and be "altogether a task for a god in every way" (246a). Instead, he proposes to say "about [the soul's] structure" (περὶ δὲ τῆς ἰδέας αὐτῆς) merely "what it is like" by using an image (246a–256e). Interestingly, he uses language reminiscent of the organic unity in myth of intrinsically dissimilar kinds of thing that we saw in the *Republic* image, calling the soul a "natural union (συμφύτῳ δυνάμει) of a team of winged horses and their charioteer" (246a). He goes on to draw a contrast between chariot teams that the gods have and those that "we" have:

> The gods have horses and charioteers that are themselves all good and come from good stock besides, while everyone else has a mixture. To begin with, our driver is in charge of a pair of horses; second, one of his horses is beautiful and good and from stock of the same sort, while the other is the opposite and has the opposite sort of bloodline. This means that chariot-driving in our case is inevitably a painfully difficult business. (246a–b)

While we may readily assume that the three-part metaphor for the soul in this image aligns with the tripartite account of the soul from the *Republic*, Socrates never actually identifies the white horse as the spirited part and the black horse as the appetitive part. He does, however, explicitly identify the chariot driver as νοῦς (247c). As with the image in the *Republic*, one intuitively pictures oneself as this driver rather than one of the horses or the chariot team as a whole. When Socrates says that the chariot-driving is difficult, we picture ourselves having a rough time steering the horses. Again, this feature of the image seems propaideutic, subtly encouraging us to alienate certain aspects of our psychology from ourselves and thereby enter into the philosophical life.

At the climax of the soul's journey the charioteer gains a glimpse of "the Beings" (presumably the forms) provided that he follows the appropriate god closely. The horses, however, do not gain this vision. Since this glimpse of the Beings in the past is meant to explain our present ability to "understand speech in terms of general forms, proceeding to bring many perceptions together into a reasoned unity" (249c), we naturally imagine ourselves within the story from the perspective of the charioteer who has the necessary experience rather than from the perspective of the horses who do not. In principle, someone might think that our current ability to "understand speech in terms of general forms" might belong to the whole soul in virtue of one of its parts having the appropriate prenatal experience. I find it quite difficult, however, to imagine myself within the myth from the perspective of the chariot team considered as a whole, or again, to imagine the chariot team considered as a whole possessing the cognitive ability to "understand speech in terms of general forms." This does not prove much about Plato's considered psychology, however, since it is, after all, only an image. What it does show, however, is that Socrates is capable of using the imaginative force of his images to push his audience toward one way of conceiving themselves rather than others.

On the other side of things, we may consider that the struggle between the driver and the black horse is a struggle for control, a struggle over the direction that the whole chariot team will take. And the answer to the question "What sort of being am I, divided or unified, savage or gentle, bestial or divine?" hangs in the balance. The whole myth of the chariot team tells us about a fall from an ideal condition. Surely we are meant to learn from this narrative that the kind of soul that we ourselves are lies open to threats from within. We are not like the gods who maintain consistently an ideal mode of life but rather are capable of slipping down into a condition where the steersman νοῦς does not enjoy perfect control. We find ourselves in this life, then, faced with the challenge of regaining a certain identity, an identity in which νοῦς wins mastery. Again, that this mastery means victory *for us* points to an ideal identification between the self and νοῦς, but the contingency of this victory points to a less than ideal distance between the self and νοῦς.

Core Personalist Ideas

In the last chapter, we saw that personalism owed an important debt to Platonic thinking about the soul even while cautioning against some of the dangers inherent in dualistic thinking. Again in this chapter, I will argue that three core personalist ideas develop straight out of Platonic thinking about the tripartite soul. Before that development within the tradition takes place, however, we can also spot again some important shortcomings and potential pitfalls. First, the tripartite conception of self-mastery is an important antecedent for personalist conceptions of freedom, although Plato lacks a developed account of the will as a distinct faculty. Second, the distinction between faulty and ideal configurations of soul lays the groundwork for a distinction between two conceptions of what it means to be a person, one given in our very essence, the other achieved through our responsible agency. Third, the emphasis on the inner workings of our own soul turns the philosophical project toward "interiority" and away from an exclusively "cosmological" conception of man with which we saw Karol Wojtyła finding fault in the first chapter.

Freedom and Self-Mastery—In an important chapter of *Transformation in Christ*, Dietrich von Hildebrand argues that Christian transformation involves a process of coming fully awake rather than remaining in the somnolence of what he calls "false consciousness."[24] Only by doing so can a person achieve full moral agency because one must be truly conscious of the objective world of values in order to make a free moral response. His account of a radical personal freedom in this chapter is representative of personalist convictions and shows signs of both continuity with and development of several features of the tripartite account of soul:

> [True consciousness] is the awakening to full moral majority, the discovery of the capacity of sanctioning. The behavior of *unconscious* persons is dictated by their nature. They tacitly identify themselves with whatever response their nature suggests to them. They have not yet discovered the

---

24. Hildebrand, "True Consciousness," in *Transformation in Christ*.

possibility of emancipating themselves, by virtue of their free personal center, from their nature; they make no use as yet of this primordial capacity inherent in the personal mode of being. Hence their responses to values, even when they happen to be adequate, will always have something accidental about them.[25]

While the metaphysical structure of personal existence is not the focal theme of this passage, I want to draw attention to several of the rich details that suggest the background metaphysical picture that Hildebrand is working with.

First, we have the "capacity of sanctioning." Throughout Hildebrand's ethical writings we often return to the theme of response. The world outside our head is replete with real values, some moral, others aesthetic, intellectual, or ontological. While not completely identical, these "values" in Hildebrand's philosophy bear a close resemblances to Plato's forms, as we will examine in more detail in the next chapter. Like the forms, values are real, mind-independent, intelligible objects. The beauty of Beethoven's ninth symphony, the goodness inherent in a father's act of forgiveness toward his son, the bond between two friends, or the health restored to an old woman after an illness are all really valuable whether a particular person subjectively finds them so or not. These objective values appear for us in subjective experience and by so appearing place a call upon our lives, inviting us toward an adequate mode of response. The beauty of Beethoven's ninth may call us to admiration, while the goodness of a father's forgiveness may call us likewise to forgive.

At the root of all these different modes of response, however, lies the same inner "yes" to value. Before I can step out and truly forgive my son, I must first see forgiveness and say within myself, "Yes, this is good; this is what I must do." By doing so, I *sanction* my act of forgiveness, and it becomes an act that *I* perform rather than something that merely happens *to me* or *within me*.[26] Hildebrand calls this a "primordial capacity

---

25. Ibid., 62.
26. For a further development of this contrast between what *I do* and what happens *to me* and the correspondence between this and the person–nature contrast, see Crosby, *The Selfhood of the Human Person*, chapter 3, section 2.

inherent in the personal mode of being," because this capacity forms part of the fundamental difference between persons and non-persons. Cats and trees do not have the capacity to stand back from the organic processes directing their existence. Human persons, by contrast, live in a fundamentally richer mode of being.

We might see a certain kinship between this Hildebrandian insight and the Platonic idea that only certain souls can enter a human being, souls that have had a preincarnate vision of the forms and thus possess mind (νοῦς). There is a difference, however, between Hildebrand's insistence on a *volitional* center proper to the personal mode of existence and the basically *epistemic* center that we find in the rational element of the tripartite scheme. A volitional freedom of this part may be implied (especially in *Republic* 443c–d, discussed above), but it is never made explicit much less centrally thematized. In short, the tripartite model simply lacks the later conception of the *will*.[27] Later Platonists, especially St. Augustine, do incorporate a robust conception of will while maintaining continuity with the larger Platonic model, but in order to do so they must borrow the Stoic conception of the ἡγεμονικόν, a conscious center capable of saying "yes" or "no" to impressions.[28]

Next, we have, according to Hildebrand, the notion that unconscious persons "tacitly identify themselves" with the responses dictated by their nature. While we have the capacity to stand back from it, we do possess a nature, including the organic processes that direct our actions like other animals, and we do not always exercise our higher capacity. As an embodied animal we feel the urge to eat or the urge to run from danger, even though as conscious persons we are under no necessity to act upon these urges. We can observe them and decide not to eat or not to run—even unto death. Those who are morally sleepwalking, however, experience little gap between natural impulse and action. They are carried along, according to Hildebrand, on the stream of natural causality and experience their lives as something happening to them rather than something they

---

27.. For extensive discussion see Albrecht Dihle, *The Theory of Will in Classical Antiquity* (Berkeley: University of California Press, 1982).

28. This is the central thesis of Michael Frede in *A Free Will*.

are doing. As they are carried along, the *I* that is capable of standing back from the steam of impulses grows quieter and quieter until it becomes submerged in the automatism of organic psychic processes. Hence, the *I* that they take themselves to be becomes more and more mistakenly identified with the stream of impulses itself. The glutton identifies with his craving; the coward identifies with his cowardice. This identification must be "tacit" because the very act of articulating an identity between the self and the stream of natural impulses begins to make manifest the existence of a self that can stand back from the stream.

The shallowness of a life lived in this way remains, according to Hildebrand, even when we consider those cases where the impulses arising from nature drive us toward actions that we would and ought to sanction from our free personal center. We are inclined, perhaps, to sympathize with someone in pain or to seek companionship. Even the beasts do such things, but they do them without the explicit conscious agency of a moral person. When we do what we ought to do merely because we are carried along by our impulses rather than because we recognize that we ought to do it and assent to the moral value involved, we too live as if we were beasts. We begin to identify with one aspect of ourselves at the expense of another, the aspect of ourselves that operates according to organic causality as opposed to the aspect that operates according to consciously perceived reasons for acting.

This notion of "identifying with" either lower impulses or higher reasons is thoroughly Platonic. It could have been lifted straight from the image of the farmer, lion, and beast in the *Republic*, and sounds much like our discussion of the "moving spotlight" view of identity that we discussed above. Indeed, it was this ethical imperative to conform to λόγος rather than impulse that animated so much of the early Christian adoption of Platonic psychology, especially in the early monastic movements.[29]

Nevertheless, there is a subtlety here that needs careful examination. In Hildebrand's conception of the "free personal center," we importantly

---

29. Numerous examples can be found, for example, throughout the *Philokalia*, ed. G. E. H. Palmer, Philip Sherard, Kallistos Ware (New York: Farrar, Straus and Giroux, 1983).

possess a capacity to stand back from *nature*. In the tripartite account of soul, it is not altogether clear where the rational part sits with respect to nature, although there are hints throughout the dialogues of a similar conception. In the *Phaedo*, Socrates expresses dissatisfaction with Anaxagoras, who proposed to explain everything in terms of Νοῦς but then proceeds only to give explanations in terms of natural, mechanical causes (96a–99d). Socrates demonstrates the absurdity of this by comparing it to a mechanical, natural explanation of his own actions. If his actions are to be explained in terms of his mind, he says, they must instead be explained by an appeal to what he thinks is best. Perhaps as an attempt to correct this failing in Anaxagoras, the discussion of the construction of the cosmos in the *Timaeus* is divided between the works of Νοῦς and the works of Ἀνάγκη (necessity, fate). Finally, the Myth of Er describes individual souls in a mystical realm somehow standing back from and observing the "Spindle of Ἀνάγκη" (616b–c) and in this space making their all-important choice of lives. As we will discuss more fully in the next chapter, noetic souls are conceived as occupying a middle position that is obscured by the freshmen version of Platonic ontology as divided strictly between Being and Becoming. In some way, the highest part of the soul allows us to stand back from the deterministic chain of natural causality (the domain of Becoming, nature, and fate) because we are capable of acting from a source outside that chain (the domain of Being, the forms, and the divine).

Finally, Hildebrand's language of "emancipating" ourselves from the dictates of our nature by virtue of our "free personal center" brings the theme of freedom versus slavery to the fore. The constant submission to the impulses given by our more bestial impulses appear as a form of slavery to a tyrannical master. The dawning consciousness of the distinction between my free personal center and these natural impulses is a kind of waking up. The exertion of the capacity to sanction or renounce what comes from impulse is a liberation from prison. For all this to make any sense, this free personal center must have a better claim to being the real self than the impulses that it overcomes, and this was exactly the force of the multiple discussions of self-control that we examined above, and the theme of spiritual emancipation through progressive identification with mind is a central Platonic concern. Hence, there is a close link between the Platonic conception of intrapsychic self-mastery and a personalist account of inner personal freedom.

Achievement of Identity—In *Liturgy and Personality*, Hildebrand draws a strong distinction between "person" and "personality," that is again representative of an important strand in personalist thought. On the one hand, personalists claim that every human being, just by being a human being, is a person, someone rather than something, an altogether distinct mode of being, in virtue of which the person possesses an infinite worth and dignity. This is, perhaps, *the* defining proposition of personalist philosophies. On the other hand, personalists often claim that persons are called to develop as persons, a calling that we frequently fail to fulfill. Hildebrand explains the contrast thus:

> In speaking of personality as distinct from the person, we have in mind something clearly defined. Every man is a person in that his being is essentially conscious; and he is a subject who enters into relations with others, and who knows, wills, and loves. A person is a being who "possesses himself," who does not simply exist but who actively achieves his being, and has the power to choose freely. But every man is not a personality. Only persons can be personalities, but in order to be a personality it is not enough just to be a person.[30]

The achievement of personality is, according to Hildebrand, the fulfillment of an ideal type, living up to the fullness of what it means to be a person.

> A personality in the true sense of the word is the man who rises above the average only because he fully realizes the *classical human* attitudes, because he knows more deeply and originally than the average man, loves more profoundly and authentically, wills more clearly and correctly than the others, makes full use of his freedom; in a word—the complete, profound, true man.[31]

---

30. Dietrich von Hildebrand, *Liturgy and Personality* (Steubenville, OH: Hildebrand Press, 2016), 13.

31. Ibid., 13–14.

As in the previous discussion, we see a close resemblance to Platonic ideas—perhaps it is even resemblance between ancestor and offspring—while we also see important developments. On the tripartite account, as we have examined, we do have a basic kind of soul that none of us could fail to be, the kind of souls that have seen the forms, that is, the kind of souls with νοῦς. We also have an ideal of progressive achievement of identity by identifying more and more fully with νοῦς, thereby subordinating the lower aspects of the soul. On both counts, however, the picture lays the emphasis on the epistemic dimension and leaves underdeveloped—though by no means entirely absent—the elements of love, will, and affectivity that Hildebrand insists upon.

If the language were updated, one could see one of Plato's characters saying, "Every man is a person in that his being is essentially conscious." But what would Plato make of the further claim, "He is a subject who enters into relations with others"? The ideal of the classical personality for Hildebrand includes not only that such a man "knows more deeply" but also that he "loves more profoundly and authentically" and "wills more clearly and correctly."

To be sure, no one can deny that ἔρως is a central theme in the Platonic dialogues, and the affectivity associated with erotic encounter is pivotal in the ascent of the soul. At the very beginning of the Ladder of Love in the *Symposium*, it is the erotic encounter with the beloved that kicks off the whole spiritual ascent, and Ἔρως personified as a mediating spirit is the "leader" that guides the soul up to the final vision of beauty itself (210a–211d). Similarly in the *Phaedrus*, the philosophical soul that has lost its wings and fallen into our human, embodied condition, is first stirred awake and begins to regrow its wings at the erotic sight of the "godlike face" of its beloved (251a). The description Socrates gives of the soul regrowing its wings includes a moving poetic description of affectivity, an affectivity that is not opposed to but, rather, constitutive of the redemption of the soul.

Nevertheless, one might well wonder whether the pederastic conception of love in these two passages would satisfy Hildebrand's desire for a thoroughgoing philosophy of interpersonal relations and his demand, in

The Heart, that we give affectivity its due. Other types of relationships are much less central in the dialogues and the person is hardly conceived as a being that is *essentially* relational. Ἔρως, with all its affective dimension, is certainly a driving force in the Platonic ascent, but it is hard to see how other forms of affectivity are to be located in the tripartite account. While each of the three parts of the soul are frequently defined by their loves,[32] one gets the distinct impression that most forms of human affectivity would count as πάθη and be assigned to the lower two parts of the soul. This would render most forms of human affectivity mortal elements of our embodied psychic condition. At best, such elements are good in their place but in need of subordination to our immortal element and ultimately extrinsic to our true self. At worst, such elements are an obstacle to the Platonic project of ascent. This leaves the Platonic tradition with an overly intellectualist conception of the ideal "personality" toward which we are to strive, as though the perfected person is ultimately just a bare mind—a position that Plato strongly hints at several times in the passages we will examine in the next chapter but which Plotinus makes fully explicit (for example, in *Enneads* 1.1, 5.3, and 5.8). Admittedly, this mind is not a cold, Vulcan reason but a mind burning with an ἔρως for eternal beauty. Even so, this would not satisfy the personalist desire for an account of a complete *human* personality.

Focus on Interiority—In chapter 1, we examined Karol Wojtyła's description of the Aristotelian definition of the human being as exclusively "cosmological." A cosmological conception of man sees him from the outside, a specimen of a certain natural kind, with a given place in an ordered cosmos. By contrast, personalist thinking, according to Wojtyła, turns toward the "interiority" of man. Without minimizing the truth in the cosmological account, a personalist account would give man's subjectivity and inner experience its full due, seeing the dimension of man that is irreducible to the realm of nature. Surprisingly, Wojtyła remarks that this other way of looking at the human being is "just as old as the need for reduction in Aristotle's definition," but he does not specify what other

32. See Charles H. Kahn, "Plato's Theory of Desire," *The Review of Metaphysics* 41, no. 1 (1987): 77–130.

thinkers or texts of the period he has in mind.[33] My own contention is that the Platonic tradition has historically provided an interior-oriented way of thinking about ourselves that runs in parallel to the more "cosmological" conceptions that see man from the outside.

One might be forgiven for thinking, based on a few limited passages from the myths, that Plato's conception of souls is just as "cosmological" as Aristotle's definition of human beings. In the *Timaeus*, for example, we are given an outside-in picture of our souls in the cosmos. Certainly, "souls" are frequently treated as one kind of entity alongside other kinds of entity, viewed from the outside, and situated in an orderly, top-down conception of the universe. This picture does differ from the Aristotelian definition with which Wojtyła takes issue by placing the emphasis on what it means to be a certain kind of immortal, ethereal being rather than what it means to belong to a certain kind of animal species. While perhaps more mysterious in character, this way of thinking about ourselves as a collection of wispy entities whirling around in a great cosmic dance is no less external.

Nevertheless, the mythic descriptions of souls from the outside is not the end of the story. (To be fair to Aristotle, his definition of man is not the end of the story for him either.) The central thrust of many Platonic dialogues is to push the interlocutors to make an inward turn. While different pictures of the cosmos are sometimes given, priority is always given to the philosophical quest, and this means an interior-oriented approach to the soul's redemption.

This interior-oriented approach is driven by the tripartite conception of the soul. The whole point of tripartition is to give an explanation for our struggles in terms of a conflict that goes on inside our own souls. This stands in contrast to philosophies that explain our predicament in terms of a struggle against the exterior world, cosmic forces, the gods, or even our own body. Reference to all these exterior conflicts can certainly be found in the dialogues, but ultimately the tripartite account of the soul turns our attention inward. It causes me to conceive my deepest

---

33. Wojtyła, "Subjectivity and the Irreducible in the Human Being."

problems as problems inside my own psyche. The solution to these problems involves the first step of self-knowledge. I cannot begin to untangle my psyche and subordinate the lower elements to the higher if I do not know what elements there are and what their nature is. Hence, Socrates again and again insists in several dialogues that the beginning of the philosophical quest is obedience to the Delphic Oracle. As Socrates tells Phaedrus, he thinks it is ridiculous to inquire about exterior questions of the cosmos if he does not yet know himself (229e). He therefore undertakes the philosophical quest, which means for him that he turns away from looking into those external things and instead looks into his own self to figure out the inner complexities of his own soul (230a, discussed above). The philosophical quest, however, only *begins* with this self-knowledge. Even after the elements of the soul have been identified, there comes the long struggle within oneself to subordinate the lower to the higher, the adventitious to the essential.

A confirmation of how central this interior-oriented approach is to the dialogues is the somewhat greater emphasis on interiority that we consistently find in the Platonic tradition in contrast to other ancient schools of thought. Consider, for example, distinctly Platonic themes of self-knowledge, the philosophical life as care for one's own soul, the injunction to turn "toward the inside" (εἰς τὸ εἴσω) to find the eternal within one's own soul, all based on a tripartite conception of our interior struggle. Contrast this with the space devoted to questions of physics, biology, meteorology, natural history, or the externals of human affairs in other schools. I do not mean to paint this contrast in too bold a light. There was much borrowing between the Platonists, the Peripatetics, the Stoics, and even the Epicureans in the classical period, and the other schools, especially the Stoics do have their own discussions of our subjectivity and interior life. Nevertheless, every time we sample Platonic authors throughout history we consistently find a recognizable flavor that savors of interiority. Consider, for example, the inward-oriented themes that dominate the landscape when we turn to Plotinus, Iamblichus, St. Augustine, St. Gregory of Nyssa, Proclus, St. Maximus the Confessor, right down to Ficino or Thomas Taylor.

In the next chapter, we will see how this whole inward-orientation ultimately centers around a divine element in our souls and hence motivates a quest for reunion with the divine. Already, however, we are in a position to see how the tripartite account of soul generates a kind of proto-personalist set of concerns that exert a steady philosophical pressure toward thinking about and wrestling with our interior life.

CHAPTER 4

Nous, Divinity, and *Theosis*

But it is not possible, Theodorus, that evil should be destroyed—for there must always be something opposed to the good; nor is it possible that it should have its seat in heaven. But it must inevitably haunt human life, and prowl about this earth. That is why a man should make all haste to escape from earth to heaven; and escape means becoming as like God (ὁμοίωσις θεῷ) as possible; and a man becomes like God when he becomes just and pious, with understanding (μετὰ φρονήσεως). (*Theaetetus* 176a–b)[1]

ACCORDING TO A COMMON INTERPRETATION, Plato holds that all reality can be divided into the eternal forms, on the one hand, and their concrete participants, on the other: the realm of Being over the realm of Becoming; the divine over the mortal. When we hold to this "two-worlds" schematization too dogmatically, however, it becomes difficult to see where he would locate the true self. We find many texts indicating that the soul, especially the rational aspect of the soul, plays an *intermediary* role in the total picture. At the risk of oversimplifying,

---

1. Trans. M. J. Levett as revised by Myles Burnyeat.

we can sketch an alternative interpretation of Platonic ontology that includes this intermediary as a third layer. Such a picture would include three distinct ontological categories: (i) the forms, the timeless principles of intelligibility; (ii) concrete particulars, the immediately intelligible objects, manifestations of the former principles of intelligibility into space and time; and (iii) rational souls, the living noetic centers receptive to this intelligibility, attendant to and responsible for things that come to be and pass away yet rooted outside space and time because of their receptivity to the transcendent grounds of intelligibility. By actively imitating the intelligible principles governing the motions of the cosmos, the rational soul becomes ever more assimilated to its ground and ever more receptive to it. Throughout the dialogues, the principles of intelligibility are called "divine" both because of their transcendent nature and because of the grounding role they play in the total cosmology. Insofar as the rational soul becomes ever more receptive to this ground we may call it "divine" in an analogous sense, and it is in this analogous sense that we can understand the various references we find in the dialogues to νοῦς, τὸ λογιστικόν, or "immortal soul" as something divine within us.

By drawing our attention to this three-layer picture I also hope to undermine those interpretations that locate the true self within the two-layer picture wholly on the side of the divine. I can find no text in the dialogues that identifies the self with a form, with Universal Reason, or with God.[2] I do find, however, a number of passages that connect the self in a deep and essential way with the forms, with reason, and with the divine.

Often enough in Greek, "divine" (θεῖος) is a term in contrast to "mortal" or "human." In Homer, we humans are the mortals (βροτοί, θνητοί), while the gods are untouched by our ills, destined never to die. The gods are *not us*. Being divine means being *not human*, belonging to a sphere elevated above the mortal plane. In chapter 2, we saw Socrates use this

---

2. For the idea that there is a form of self see R. E. Allen, "Note on Alcibiades i, 129b 1," *The American Journal of Philology* 83, no. 2 (1962): 187–90, at 189. For the identification of the self with Universal Reason see Richard Sorabji, *Self*, 2, 6, 34–35, 115. For the identification of the true self with God see Annas, "Self Knowledge in Early Plato," 111–38, at 129–31, and David M. Johnson, "God as the True Self: Plato's Alcibiades i," 3.

common opposition between being human and being divine in the contrasting pairs of the Kinship Argument. We also saw, however, that Socrates surprisingly locates *us* on the side of the divine rather than on the side of the human. In this chapter we will try to make sense of this. To do so, however, we must be careful about how we use the word "divine."

I want to distinguish a number of senses in which we might call something "divine." First and most obviously, we might say that something is divine in a *strict* sense, that it is numerically identical to God or a god.

Second, we might say that something is divine in a *material* or *partial* sense, that it is made out of God or a god or a part of either. This sense lies behind the idea, somewhat common in the ancient world, that we all contain a divine spark, a little piece of some great reservoir of god-stuff. At *Philebus* 29b–30d, for example, Socrates argues that each of the elements within us are just a tiny portion of what is in the cosmos as a whole. Just as the fire or earth in us is a tiny portion of the fire or earth in the universe, so too our soul is a tiny portion of soul in the universe. A similar material or partial sense can be found in the famous mixing bowl image of the *Timaeus* in which human souls are made from the leftover ingredients that composed the World Soul (41d).³

Third, we might say that something is divine in an *analogous* sense, that it somehow mirrors or reflects God or a god. Christian authors frequently have this sense in mind when they invoke the idea that we are made in the image of God. Similarly, we see the idea of becoming like God (ὁμοίωσις θεῷ) in the passage from the *Theaetetus* with which we began (176a–b). The notions of imitation, likeness, participation, and analogy are, of course, central to the entire Platonic metaphysics. On pain of the Third Man Argument of Aristotle or the Likeness Regress in the *Parmenides*, however, any ultimately coherent Platonic metaphysics must develop a conception of analogy or imitation that has two crucial features:

---

3. Another good example can be found in Epictetus's *Discourses* 1.1.10–12, where Zeus gives Epictetus a portion of himself by giving him the power of choice, or again *Discourses* 2.8.11, where Epictetus claims that we all contain a particle of God within us.

1. Analogy is asymmetrical, that is, can be analogous to without being analogous to , and

2. Analogy is independent of any univocally shared quality, that is, can be analogous to without there being *any* property such that is and is *in the same sense*.

Whether Plato himself arrives at an ultimately coherent Platonic metaphysics is, of course, a crux of interpretation. While I believe that he does, we need consider here only what is at stake for the conception of analogy in the dialogues.

Fourth, we might say that something is divine in a *qualitative* sense, that it possesses a quality central to what it means to be God or a god (again, in a non-univocal sense). Someone might exclaim, for instance, that a painting is "simply divine" because it captures a certain kind of beauty. Similarly in book 1 of the *Laws* (626c), Megillus addresses the Athenian Stranger by saying ὦ θεῖε, not because Megillus thinks that the Stranger is, literally, a god but because, like the gods, the Stranger evokes admiration and respect through his wisdom. While there may be much overlap between the analogous and the qualitative sense, it is helpful to distinguish cases in which something in its entirety is thought to be an analogue of God or a god from cases in which something reflects merely one aspect.

Fifth, we might say that something is divine in a *proximate* sense, that it has some contact or association with God or a god. In this way, the Greeks frequently refer to a grove, a shrine, or a particular bend in the river as divine because a god is thought to dwell there or have dealings with it in some special way. In a deeper sense, things or people are thought to take on something of the aura of the divine by drawing near. This may involve a secondary participation in some quality and so overlap with the qualitative sense above. For example, it might work like the iron in the forge, which by being in proximity with the fire comes to have the brightness of the fire in a secondary, derivative sense. But divinity by proximity need not involve any qualitative change. For example, it might work like a courtier who becomes the "royal" chamberlain, not by having any royal blood himself, but by his close association with and proximity to the king. In a famous section of the *Phaedrus* (249c), Socrates describes what happens to the soul of a philosopher:

> For just this reason it is fair that only a philosopher's mind grows wings, since its memory always keeps it as close as possible to those realities by being close to which the gods are divine (πρὸς οἷσπερ θεὸς ὢν θεῖός ἐστιν). A man who uses reminders of these things correctly is always at the highest, most perfect level of initiation, and he is the only one who is perfect as perfect can be.[4]

One might have thought that the gods were primarily divine in the strict sense simply by being gods, but Socrates says here that the gods are divine in virtue of "being close to" or simply "in relation to" (πρός) those "realities beyond heaven," that is, the Forms. Earlier, Socrates says that the success or failure of our own souls is determined by how closely each soul follows the god to which it is assigned (248a), and the theme of approach versus separation runs throughout the Palinode.

With all these senses readily available, therefore, we should not make too quick a leap into big metaphysical claims when Plato describes something in our own psychology as divine. We should pause to consider the point because an all too easy line of interpretation lies just around the corner. According to some philosophies, the true self is divine in the strict sense.[5] This perspective has far reaching philosophical ramifications, especially for monotheists. If my true self is God, your true self is God, and there is only one God, then I may infer that the distinction between my self and your self is illusory. If my true self is God, then I may begin to think that discovering myself and coming to contemplate myself turns out to be just the same as discovering and contemplating God, and vice versa. One need not look far to find such claims in various spiritual and philosophical traditions throughout the world—sometimes

---

4. Trans. Alexander Nehamas and Paul Woodruff.
5. See, for example, this claim exactly in Annas, "Self Knowledge in Early Plato," 133: "[T]he true self turns out to be God, the ultimate reality." She also comments on the frequent occurrence of this thought in the history of philosophy: "It is a thought which ... we find perennially tempting and perennially repulsive."

heavily influenced by Plato.⁶ But do we find such things explicitly written in the dialogues themselves? Do we even find such things strongly implied by the logic of arguments in the dialogues themselves? As we will see, there are many passages in the dialogues where something in us is called divine. I will argue, however, that we can make good sense of all these passages if we stick to weaker senses of "divine."

Along with the various uses of the material and qualitative senses that we have already mentioned, we must examine further the proximate and analogous sense because the typical Platonic picture of cognition imagines a kind of contact or proximity between knower and thing known by which the knower becomes a formal analogue of the thing known. An image one finds repeatedly in later Platonists is that of a signet ring (the intelligible object) being impressed into wax (the receptive intellect). Notice that in this metaphor we have analogy *because of* contact, and further notice that since the form in the wax is the inverse of the form of the signet we have exactly the kind of asymmetrical and non-univocal analogy that we required above. Since the objects of genuine knowledge are thought of as "divine" in some sense—apparently divine in a sense causally prior to the divinity of whichever gods lead the procession of souls—the knower comes to inherit the epithet "divine" by association and analogy.

We will begin, then, by examining the *Timaeus* where Timaeus and Socrates discuss cosmic Νοῦς, which we can call "divine" in the strict sense. This will make it possible to ask about the relationship between this cosmic Νοῦς and νοῦς in us. We will then examine the relationship between us and the gods in the chariot myth of the *Phaedrus* and the relationship that both we and the gods have to the forms.

---

6. Aldous Huxley, for example, identifies various versions of this idea as the central tenet of what he (rightly or wrongly) calls the perennial philosophy, Aldous Huxley, *The Perennial Philosophy* (New York: Harper, 1945). As a testament to the widespread appeal of this line of thinking in popular contemporary spirituality see the climactic scene of Paulo Coelho's *The Alchemist* (New York: HarperCollins, 1993).

Divinity and Noûs in the Timaeus

When one examines the occurrences of the terms θεός and θεῖος in the *Timaeus*, one immediately notices that they do not refer invariably to a single reality.[7] Instead, "being divine" and even "being a god" admit of degrees. As we ascend the hierarchy of being that Timaeus lays out, we find higher and higher divinities, and as we descend we find entities participating in divinity in more and more derivative ways. Alongside the medieval *scala entis* we might speak here of a *scala divinitatis*. On rung (i) of this ladder we have the Demiurge (although the model to which he looks is higher still). One step down (ii) we find the living cosmos itself. Timaeus refers to the Demiurge as the "eternal god" (ὢν ἀεὶ θεός), while he calls the universe that the Demiurge creates the "god that was yet to be" (ὁ ποτὲ ἐσόμενος θεός, 34b). Going down another step (iii), we find the great variety of gods associated with the various celestial bodies. At this stage we might plausibly suppose that Timaeus would locate the traditional Olympian deities.[8] Timaeus also mentions but does not discuss (iv) the class of *daimones* at 40d, lower than "the gods" but higher than mortal beings, and also (v) the offspring of the gods at 40d–e. Finally, he arrives at (vi) those mortal beings which nevertheless have a divine part (41a–47e). In this passage, together with its parallel at 69c–90d, we find more clearly and repeatedly than anywhere else in the Platonic corpus the idea that we human beings have something divine within us.

When he gets to the production of mortal living things, the Demiurge addresses "the gods." The Demiurge explains first that the sense in which the celestial gods are immortal is derivative rather than absolute. Because they have been bound together, they are liable to being undone. Destruction, therefore, is for them a logical possibility. But while they *can* be undone, the Demiurge promises that they *will not* be undone. The Demiurge justifies this guarantee by saying, "[W]hatever has come to be by my hands cannot be undone but by my consent," and he promises the

---

7. All translations from the *Timaeus* are from Donald J. Zeyl.
8. For example, Timaeus mentions Hermes at 38d and alludes to the standard theogonic account of the Titans and Olympians at 40d–41a.

gods that this consent will never be given. He can guarantee this latter promise because he, being perfectly good, would never consent to something evil, and the dissolution of something "well fitted together and in a fine condition" would be something evil (41a–b).

In this transition from the Demiurge to the gods, we begin to flesh out our understanding of what a derivative or diminished mode of being divine might mean. Remember that for Greek religious thinking being divine is deeply associated with being immortal. In drawing a distinction, therefore, between two modes of immortality, Timaeus also makes room for two modes of divinity. We find no hint in the text that the Demiurge and his model could fail to be. Instead, insofar as the Demiurge is that which ultimately binds together he cannot himself be something bound, and therefore is not liable to come apart by the logic of 41a. The Demiurge, then, within the structure of the myth, is immortal—and therefore divine—in an ultimate sense, while the gods are immortal—and therefore divine—in a derivative sense. This sense is derivative both because the celestial gods possess an immortality of an attenuated form and because their possession of it depends entirely upon the Demiurge. The Demiurge is immortal in himself, whereas these gods receive their divinity and immortality from him and count on his continued consent moment by moment for its maintenance.

The foregoing logic implies that only these two levels of being would exist (the Demiurge and the gods) if the Demiurge made everything himself since everything the Demiurge makes himself would be "well fitted together" and "in a fine condition." If only these two levels existed, however, there would be a gap in the plenitude of creatures that the universe ought to contain (40a, 41b–c). The Demiurge, therefore, ingeniously farms out the task of creating mortal living beings to the gods. Creatures fashioned by this lower rank of divinity are capable of being undone, perhaps because they are not as "well fitted together" as the gods and capable of winding up in something other than "a fine condition."

This process accounts for the purely mortal living things that populate the universe, but right at this stage the Demiurge inserts a striking intermediate possibility: He mentions that to some extent it will be fitting for some mortal beings "to possess something that shares our name of 'immortal'" (40c). We have, then, three senses of being immortal. Alongside our previous two, we have creatures that really are mortal yet have within them a mysterious "something" that shares the name "immortal." In order to qualify as immortal in any sense it must be made by the Demiurge himself, who then hands the "seed" off to the gods to be woven into the mortal creature (41d), but he fashions this seed from the leftover ingredients from which he made the souls of the universe and the gods. These leftovers, Timaeus says, the Demiurge mixes together only in "somewhat the same" (τινα τὸν αὐτόν) manner as those previous souls, and the mixture is not "invariably and consistently pure, but of a second and third grade of purity" (ἀκήρατα δὲ οὐκέτι κατὰ ταὐτὰ ὡσαύτως, ἀλλὰ δεύτερα καὶ τρίτα, 41d).

This "something," then, stands in an interesting intermediate position. To its glory, it is worthy of the same name, "immortal," as the Demiurge and the gods, crafted by the Demiurge himself, and made from the same basic ingredients as the Soul of the Cosmos. To its shame, however, it is not invariably and consistently pure, and it is fated, unlike the gods, to be woven together inside the casing of a mortal animal. But what exactly is this "something"? The only thing the Demiurge says in his speech to characterize it is that it is "something described as divine and ruling within those of them who always consent to follow after justice and after you [the gods]" (41c). Already, this should remind us of the rational aspect of the soul in the *Republic*, that aspect that *ought* to rule and *does* rule within "those of them who always consent to follow after justice." Within the *Timaeus* itself, however, we find more details when Timaeus returns to this theme in his second account (69c–90d). Out of all the living things in the cosmos, Timaeus says that "[the Demiurge] himself fashioned those that were divine, but assigned his own progeny the task of fashioning the generation of those that were mortal" (69c). In order to carry out their task, the gods take from the Demiurge "the immortal origin of the soul" (ἀρχὴ ψυχῆς ἀθάνατος) and encase it in the head (69c). Timaeus ultimately identifies this "something" from 40c as "reason" (λόγος, three times, 70a–b) or "mind" (νοῦς, 71b).

It would be easy for a modern reader to take the claim that reason is "the divine soul" in human beings and think that Timaeus is saying something like this: "The Demiurge, the Cosmos, and all the lower gods are rational in the sense of possessing a mode of consciousness capable of making deductive inferences. Therefore, humans are 'divine' just insofar as they too possess this mode of consciousness." This reading, however, does not capture the way the *Timaeus* consistently construes reason not in terms of consciousness and deductive inference but primarily in terms of reasonability, order, and proportion. We can find our way toward a correct reading by considering carefully several passages that connect both reason and divinity to rotation. Timaeus thinks that he can capture something about reason by using the image of circular motion, and he also thinks he can capture something about divinity with the same image. The metaphor of rotation, therefore, acts as a kind of middle term bridging the gap from what it means for something to be divine to what it means for something to be rational. The exact terms of this analogy can help us understand what exactly Timaeus means by calling νοῦς in us "the divine soul."

We first hear about circular movement when the Demiurge grants this movement to the cosmos because this movement is "suited to its body" (34a). Here, Timaeus describes rotation as "that one of the seven motions which is especially associated with understanding and intelligence" (περὶ νοῦν καὶ φρόνησιν), but he does not give any argument for this association. What he does do is simply characterize that motion as "turning continuously in the same place, spinning around upon itself" (κατὰ ταὐτὰ ἐν τῷ αὐτῷ καὶ ἐν ἑαυτῷ).[9] Later, at 37a–d, Timaeus gives an account of the cognition that takes place in the soul of the cosmos in terms of the "circles" of the Different and the Same. The former gives rise to true opinion, while the latter gives rise to understanding (νοῦς) and knowledge (ἐπιστήμη). Timaeus says that

---

9. Compare 40a–b where Timaeus describes the motions of the celestial gods as "an unvarying movement in the same place, by which the god would always think the same thoughts about the same things" (ἐν ταὐτῷ κατὰ ταὐτά, περὶ τῶν αὐτῶν ἀεὶ τὰ αὐτὰ ἑαυτῷ διανοουμένῳ).

because [the soul] circles round upon itself, whenever it comes into contact with something whose being is scatterable or else with something whose being is indivisible, *it is stirred through out its whole self.* (37a)

I have added emphasis here because the complex middle clause of this sentence may obscure the connection between the circling metaphor and the pervasive character of the soul's cognition; the former is meant in some way to explain the latter. So far, we have simply seen Timaeus use the notion of circling in connection with ideal forms of cognition, but we have yet to see *why* this one of the seven motions makes a suitable metaphor as opposed to the other six, which are characterized as "wanderings" (for example, 34a, 40b).

We may shed some light on this question if we look to a parallel passage in *Laws* 10 where the Stranger asks Clinias about the "nature of rational motion" (τίνα οὖν δὴ νοῦ κίνησις φύσιν ἔχει, 897d). Before Clinias can answer, however, the Stranger claims that the question is difficult to answer and he warns that

> [i]n answering this question we mustn't assume that mortal eyes will ever be able to look upon reason (νοῦς) and get to know it adequately: let's not produce darkness at noon, so to speak, by looking at the sun direct. We can save our sight by looking at an *image* of the object we're asking about. (897d–e)

The Stranger helps Clinias to recall the kind of motion that takes place "in a single location" and "necessarily implies continuous revolution round a central point." He claims that "this kind of motion bears the closest possible affinity and likeness to the cyclical movement of reason" (τοῦ νοῦ περίοδος, 898a). When Clinias asks (as we might also wish to do) what this image means, the Stranger replies:

> Take reason (νοῦς) on the one hand, and motion in a single location on the other. If we were to point out that in both cases the motion was (i) determined by a single plan and procedure (ἕνα λόγον καὶ τάξιν μίαν) and that it was (ii) regular (κατὰ ταὐτά), (iii) uniform (ὡσαύτως), (iv) always at the same point in space (ἐν τῷ αὐτῷ), (v) around a fixed center (περὶ τὰ

αὐτά),¹⁰ (vi) moving in the same direction (πρὸς τὰ αὐτά)¹¹ and were to illustrate both by the example of a sphere being turned on a lathe, then no one could ever show us up for incompetent makers of verbal images. (898a–b)

This enumeration of points brings out with special clarity the sense that both Timaeus and the Stranger want to associate rotation with *stability* and *consistency*. Rotation is like reason because both are consistent, providing something firm and reliable. Through this dimension of the metaphor we also see a connection with the immortality that characterizes divinity. Human life falls apart. Human beings wander and fail. The gods, however, are not subject to these ills and enjoy a life that need never stop, that abides ever the same, firm, sure, fixed.

In noticing the stability of rotation, however, we notice also a paradox. Rotation is a *motion* that gains its special character by having a center at *rest*.¹² Motion as such involves not staying the same, yet everything that the Stranger wants to emphasize about this first of all motions has to do with sameness: κατὰ ταὐτά, ἐν τῷ αὐτῷ, περὶ τὰ αὐτά, πρὸς τὰ αὐτά. This paradox rests upon an asymmetry—essential to circular motion—between the rotating body, which moves as a whole throughout, and the stable axis *about* which all this motion happens. I take it that both the Stranger and Timaeus wish to convey by this metaphor that there is an essential asymmetry between souls that have νοῦς and that which νοῦς is "about" (see the pun with περί above). Souls participating in νοῦς involve

---

10. The Stranger here plays off the cognitive ("about" a topic) and the spatial ("about" a place) meanings of the word περί. While it is true that these uses of the preposition sometimes take different cases (genitive in the former and accusative in the latter), this tendency is not absolute. See Edward N. Lee, "Reason and Rotation: Circular Movement as the Model of Mind (Nous) in Later Plato," in *Facets of Plato's Philosophy*, ed. W. H. Werkmeister (Assen: Van Gorcum, 1976), 70–102, at 76 n. 11, for argument and examples of other passages in Plato that exploit this play on meaning.

11. Accepting Lee's translation rather than Saunders's "in the same position relative to other objects." See ibid., 76 n. 12 for argument.

12. For a discussion of the essential asymmetry involved in rotation see ibid., 88–89. Lee argues that there is a striking contrast between this model of mind and that presented in so-called middle works like the *Phaedo* where cognition of forms depends on the mind becoming *like* its object (for example, the requirement that the soul be αὐτὴ καθ' αὑτήν in order to behold the forms that are αὐτὸ καθ' αὑτό at *Phaedo* 79c; see chapter 2). He further argues that this contrast need not involve Plato changing his mind but, rather, may merely signal the different rhetorical perspectives required by different dialogues.

activity—a kind of life—but the stable, regular, and measured character of this life derives from the center "about" which that life "revolves," a center that abides wholly at rest.[13] We might appeal here to the essential difference between "immortality" in the sense of everlastingness and "immortality" in the sense of atemporality. The celestial gods may be immortal by possessing an everlasting activity, but the unending character of this activity derives from the wholly atemporal center toward which that activity is directed. If we maintain our connection between divinity and immortality, then, we have discovered another sense in which the divinity of the celestial gods may be characterized as derivative. According to this interpretation, we can make better sense of what we saw Socrates say in the *Phaedrus* when he refers to "those realities by being close to which the gods are divine" (249c; see below).

This image also helps illuminate the relationship between νοῦς in the sense of cognitive act and νοῦς in the sense of virtue. In the case of circular motion, we have, on the one hand, the ongoing *activity* of the motion and, on the other, the virtuous *regularity* of the motion in virtue of which the activity participates in measure, proportion, and orderliness. We might think, for example, of the perpetual cycle of day and night. Rotation (whether we think of it as the Earth's or the sun's) imparts to this cycle the steadily fluctuating proportion of day to night and the perfectly regular measure from dawn to dawn. Human intelligence can discern these measures and proportions, and because we are capable of this discovery we find it predictable, providing a stable foundation around which we organize our life. We may even, especially if we are Greek, find an austere kind of beauty in this unstoppable, majestic dance. In the case of νοῦς, recall that νοῦν ἔχειν means "to be reasonable," and that Plato often uses νοῦς alongside other virtue terms like σοφία to indicate that feature of a person or a system that accounts for measure, proportion, and orderliness (all of which are understood as the *best* way for things to be). Just as the rotation of the sphere imposes a determinate order upon

---

13. For the connection between the rotation metaphor and the idea that νοῦς involves activity see ibid., 86. Lee argues that this marks a shift from understanding νοῦς as a state (for example, φρόνησις described as a πάθημα at *Phaedo* 79d).

everything connected to it, the activity of νοῦς concerning its object imposes a determinate order on everything that it governs.

By understanding the several senses in which the gods themselves are characterized in the *Timaeus* as possessing a derivative sense of divinity and by understanding the connection between the divine activity of νοῦς and rotation, we are now in a position to understand the even more derivative sense of divinity in human beings by looking at the presence of νοῦς in the human soul and the interference that "wandering" linear motions cause to its circular motion. Again, Timaeus relies on the metaphor of circular motion to connect conceptual threads that may otherwise remain disconnected. As just one example of how far he exploits this metaphor, Timaeus even explains the physical shape of the head in terms of the gods "copying the revolving shape of the universe." The head, he asserts, is "the most divine part of us, and master of all our other parts" (44d). In this description, even a physical part of a mortal organism is described as "divine" in virtue of its connection with circular motion and the role that it plays in housing the divine part of the soul. Timaeus again appeals to the notion of imitating the rotating movements in the cosmos a few pages later when he describes the "supreme good" that eyesight offers when it turns us toward philosophy:

> The god invented sight and gave it to us so that we might observe the orbits of intelligence (νοῦς) in the universe and apply them to the revolutions of our own understanding (διανόησις). For there is a kinship between them, even though our revolutions are disturbed, whereas the universal orbits are undisturbed. So once we have come to know them and to share in the ability to make correct calculations according to nature, we should stabilize the straying revolutions within ourselves by imitating the completely unstraying revolutions of the god. (47b–c)

This passage alone should challenge the notion that there is a strong numerical identity between the rational part of the soul and Universal Reason.[14] In this description we find a clear distinction between "our

---

14. See Sorabji, *Self*, 2, 6, 34–35, 115, for this thesis. Robert W. Hall, "Ψυχή as Differentiated Unity in the Philosophy of Plato," *Phronesis* 8, no. 1 (1963): 63–82, at 64, discusses this view, which he calls "the traditional approach" to the question of the identity of the immortal soul.

own understanding" and the "intelligence in the universe." Our whole trouble, in fact, stems from a misalignment of these two. And our goal is not to *merge with* the noetic activity of the World Soul but to *imitate* it.[15] All this is possible, however, because the two are "akin" (συγγενεῖς) to one another. Something in us is capable of "rotation" in the sense of an activity deriving its stable character from its centeredness on its fixed, unitary object. This kinship remains even when we take into account that the mixture of our souls from the mixing bowl is not "invariably and consistently pure, but of a second and third grade of purity" (41d). We face trouble because our revolutions are not perfectly περὶ τὰ αὐτά; they stray and they wander because they are disturbed. Our goal, however, is to apply our astronomical observations correctly, massaging our rotations into a more and more perfect imitation of the perfect rotations we find in the heavens. Hence, we discover ourselves as caught between two poles, as divine within the human, as immortal within the mortal. We find a certain nobility within ourselves because we are capable of an activity that reflects the divine, measured activity of the cosmos, but we also find ourselves vexed by wanderings, liable to suffer disturbances that require us to work hard at recovering the alignment we have lost.

15. My perspective here, I take it, does not ultimately disagree with the interpretation of the rotation metaphor as involving a "canceling of perspectivity," and involving "all the participating parts' full self-effacement and full reabsorption in their joint activity of circling the center" (Lee, "Reason and Rotation," 80–81). Lee argues that the image of a rotating sphere represents "a sort of concrete *unanimity* concerning the center that pervades and thus defines the entire body," and that this "conveys a compelling sense of a fully focused and yet totally distributed, or non-localized, consciousness." He calls this mode of consciousness "totally impersonal, pure 'aboutness'" (ibid., 82). I agree with him so long as "impersonal" means the cancellation of what we have previously identified as the merely conventional personae that we must shed along with our transient life and so long as "self-effacement" or "full reabsorption" means the abeyance of the idiosyncratic peculiarities of these personae. Insofar as Lee can speak of νοῦς involving "consciousness," I take it that he cannot intend his interpretation to exclude subjectivity entirely. On this point, I agree with Lloyd Gerson, *Knowing Persons*, 10, who argues that we should distinguish the idea of subjectivity from the idiosyncratic content of subjectivity and that there is no reason in principle to reject a numerical plurality of subjects all qualitatively identical because they are devoid of any idiosyncratic content, (ibid. 193, 279). I can speak of being *cognitively* "merged" with or "absorbed" in the thoughts of the universe because there is a qualitative identity of content—an alignment—while not being *ontologically* "merged" with or "absorbed" in the universe because my mind remains one thing while the universe remains another.

Our Divinity in the Phaedrus

As we saw in the last chapter, Socrates uses a myth about our state before birth, in the *Phaedrus*, riding chariots with the gods in heaven, to tell us something about ourselves now. We have already examined the ways that this myth encourages us to identify ourselves first with the ψυχή and then with the rational aspect of the ψυχή. Now we must consider the ways that this myth encourages us to think of our true selves as "divine." The myth does not claim that we are divine in the strict sense, but instead our souls are clearly distinguished throughout from the procession-leading gods, on the one hand, and from the forms, on the other (here referred to simply as "the beings" or "the realities," τὰ ὄντα). The sense in which we are "divine" in the myth is much weaker: simply that in our original condition we are *in the presence of* the gods and the forms, and thereby *receptive to* intelligible reality. We can be numbered among that company, albeit on a much lower rank. Further, at the height of our journey we not only behold the forms, we are also nourished by them. This requires that our souls must be doubly fitted to the forms. First, we must be so constituted so as to be able to behold them. Second, we must be constituted such that this beholding is *good for us* as food is good for our bodies.

As he begins to recount his remarkable chariot image, Socrates contrasts the souls of the gods with the souls of "everyone else" (246b). The gods have only good horses (notice that Socrates does not say just how many) and charioteers, while "everyone else" has a mixture. We are meant to place ourselves in this latter class because, in the next sentence, Socrates says that "our" driver is in charge of one good and one bad horse (246b). We further learn about the gods that it is "pure fiction" to say that they are immortal beings composed of body and soul because a soul–body composite could not be immortal "on any reasonable account" (246c). This aside relies on the traditional axiom of Greek religious thinking that being divine means being immortal, but Socrates' tale has expanded the class of immortal beings from the gods proper to "all soul" (245c–246c), even when a particular soul shows up for a time as the principle animating a composite mortal organism. In this sense, our souls—which is to say *we ourselves*—are really immortal and therefore divine, although we do not belong to the ranks of the gods who lead the procession because our immortal souls are prone to falling into mortal organisms while theirs are not.

Along with immortality we also learn about heaven as Socrates structures the myth around a basic spatial polarity between up and down. The wings of a soul naturally carry it "aloft," which is "where the gods all dwell" (246d). Hence, out of all physical organs, wings are "akin to the divine" (246e). The gods and their followers undergo a cyclical journey of ascent and return, but the emphasis of the myth is on the goodness of the upward trajectory, led by Zeus, as opposed to the downward fall, occasioned by the heaviness, rebellion, and unmanagability of our bad horses. Hence, we have a picture of heaven, the divine space, as "up there" and a picture of earth, the mortal human space, as "down here." The thing that makes heaven such a good place, however, does not lie within heaven's own borders, despite its "many wonderful places" (247a). Instead, we learn about a mysterious "place beyond heaven." We want to go *up* in heaven because its uppermost limit, the "rim of heaven," looks out upon something else (247b–c).

What, then, is this something else? How should we imagine it within the myth? Socrates describes it thus:

> What is in this place is without color and without shape and without solidity, a being that really is what it is (οὐσία ὄντως οὖσα), the subject of all true knowledge, visible only to intelligence, the soul's steersman (ψυχῆς κυβερνήτῃ μόνῳ θεατὴ νῷ). Now a god's mind is nourished by intelligence and pure knowledge (θεοῦ διάνοια νῷ τε καὶ ἐπιστήμῃ ἀκηράτῳ τρεφομένη), as is the mind of any soul that is concerned to take in what is appropriate to it, and so it is delighted at last to be seeing what is real and watching what is true, feeding on all this and feeling wonderful, until the circular motion brings it around to where it started. On the way around it has a view of Justice as it is; it has a view of Self-control; it has a view of Knowledge —not the knowledge that is close to change, that becomes different as it knows the different things which we consider real down

here. No, it is the knowledge of what really is what it is (τὴν ἐν τῷ ὅ ἐστιν ὂν ὄντως ἐπιστήμην). And when the soul has seen all the things that are as they are (τὰ ὄντα ὄντως) and feasted on them, it sinks back inside heaven and goes home. (247c–e)

As we saw in chapter 4, Socrates does us the service of explicitly identifying the steersman of the chariot as νοῦς, the aspect of the soul to which the realities beyond heaven are visible (ψυχῆς κυβερνήτῃ μόνῳ θεατὴ νῷ; 247c). In the very next sentence, however, Socrates seems to identify the very same aspect of the soul as διάνοια and uses νοῦς (along with ἐπιστήμη) to refer to that which nourishes the mind. Νοῦς, therefore, does double duty as a term, referring to both subject and object. On the one hand, νοῦς refers to that intelligible object glimpsed by the soul beyond heaven and, on the other, to the soul considered as a subject suitably receptive to that intelligibility. In a similar way, Socrates names ἐπιστήμη as one of the realities that the soul beholds, but it also seems to name (although not explicitly in this paragraph) the resulting experience or state in the soul that does the beholding. The minds of the gods are definitely nourished by this experience, but there seems to be some question about the minds of other souls, for Socrates qualifies what he says by restricting it to "any soul that is concerned to take in what is appropriate to it" (247d). At the least, however, this experience is open to souls besides the gods, and there is a relationship of aptness between the realities beheld and any mind capable of beholding.

We can learn something about the nourishment of the mind by the realities it beholds if we look back to the way Socrates uses a similar idea of nourishment in connection with the soul's wings. As we saw, Socrates says that wings are "akin to the divine, which has beauty, wisdom, goodness, and everything of that sort." These things possessed by what is divine "nourish the soul's wings, which grow best in their presence; but foulness and ugliness make the wings shrink and disappear" (246e). To generalize, the idea seems to be that if X is akin to Y, X will be nourished by the presence of what Y has. Again the underlying idea seems to be that the kinship between X and Y means that what is proper to Y will be suitable to or good for X. Conversely, what is opposed to Y will be harmful to or even destructive of X.

Turning back to our central passage, Socrates uses four verbs connected with eating: (i) "nourished," (ii) "take in," (iii) "feeding on," and (iv) "feasting" (247d–e). These verbs are interwoven with six verbs connected with sight: (i) "seeing," (ii) "watching," (iii–v) "has a view" (three times), (vi) "seen" (247d–e). Throughout, the objects of both sets of verbs seem to be one and the same, that is, the "beings" beyond heaven. We have, then, a twofold relation between the mind and these realities being characterized by the metaphors of gazing upon and feeding upon. Both metaphors depend upon the idea of receptivity and suitability. For sight, the eye is specifically receptive to colors, but not receptive to tones. Hence, colors are appropriate to the eye in a way that tones are not. We might say that the eye has a certain affinity for or kinship with colors, and this is not erased when we notice that colors and eyes are wholly different kinds of things. Likewise, racehorses are nourished best by grass grown on Kentucky limestone. Their bones grow strong and they flourish to their full potential on farms where they can regularly take this in. Again, we might say that racehorses have a certain affinity for or kinship with Kentucky grass even though a horse is not a kind of grass and perhaps the two have no relevant properties in common. Socrates' brief explanation in the next paragraph confirms this connection between the seeing and eating metaphors and a receptivity in the soul to that which is suitable to and good for it:

> The reason there is so much eagerness to see the plain where truth stands is that this pasture has the grass that is the right food for the best part of the soul, and it is the nature of the wings that lift up the soul to be nourished by it. (248b–c)

The mind, then, from its perch on the rim of heaven, gazes upon and in gazing is nourished by Justice, Self-control, and Knowledge, even though it does not belong to this class of realities at all. Being "in the presence" of these realities does not involve the mind crossing over into the region beyond heaven. Instead, the presence is on the ever-moving threshold. But from this vantage point, the mind receives its special birthright, a double receptivity to what is beyond heaven, seeing and eating it.

The whole cyclical journey culminating in the act of seeing and eating Socrates calls "the life of the gods" (248a). He does not, however, limit this to the gods proper:

> As for the other souls, one that follows a god most closely, making itself most like that god, raises the head of its charioteer up to the place outside and is carried around in the circular motion with the others. (248a).

Before, at 247d, the qualification that the other souls must meet was being "concerned to take in what is appropriate." Here, souls besides those of the gods must (i) follow a god most closely and (ii) make itself most like that god. These seem to be one and the same. Emulating a god means concerning oneself with beholding and feasting upon Justice, Self-control, Knowledge, and the rest since this is the whole essence of the activity which is the divine way of life. The other souls still differ from the gods, however, in the degree and duration of their culminating vision. Socrates says that "this soul does have a view of Reality, just barely" (248a). Another kind of soul that perhaps follows its god without doing so "most" closely "rises at one time and falls at another, and because its horses pull it violently in different directions, it sees some real things and misses others" (248a). This kind of vision differs from that of the soul's god in that it is intermittent rather than steady and partial rather than complete. The final class of souls does not succeed in gaining this vision at all. Instead, they "depend on what they think is nourishment—their own opinions" (248b). As we learned in our previous discussion of the *Phaedrus*, if a soul never gains, on any cycle, a vision of that which is beyond heaven it cannot become the soul in a human soul–body composite. Our souls, therefore, must have belonged to the first or second category on at least one cycle. This marks a clear set of differences between our capacities and those of the gods proper, but it also gives a sense in which we can be called divine. We may not be gods, capable of reliably gaining and maintaining a stable and complete vision of the Beings, but we gaze and feast with the gods on the same summit because we too are noetic beings.

After enumerating the various fates of souls in the cyclic process of rebirth, Socrates gives us an important clue to his understanding of divinity when he describes what happens to the philosopher:

> For just this reason it is fair that only a philosopher's mind grows wings, since its memory always keeps it as close as possible to those realities by being close to which the gods are divine. A man who uses reminders of these things correctly is always at the highest, most perfect level of initiation, and he is the only one who is perfect as perfect can be. He stands outside human concerns and draws close to the divine; ordinary people think he is disturbed and rebuke him for this, unaware that he is possessed by god. (249c–d)

One might have thought that the gods were divine simply by being gods, but Socrates says that the gods are divine in virtue of "being close to" those realities beyond heaven. While this does not negate the differences we have already noticed between us and the gods proper, this claim means that we—insofar as we too draw close to these beings through philosophy—can participate in that very mode of life in virtue of which the gods are divine. To the extent that we do this, even while we find ourselves in a human body–soul composite, we can stand "outside human concerns." As we saw previously, all human souls are souls that at one time saw the forms and thereby are capable of understanding "speech in terms of general forms, proceeding to bring many perceptions together into a reasoned unity" (249b–c; cf. 249e). It follows, then, that all human souls have a basic potency for transcending the merely human—even if the vast majority of human souls never exercise this potency in the practice of philosophy because they face various obstacles to the act of recollection (see 250a). Someone who carries to perfection this human potential for transcending the human not only stands outside ordinary human life in his internal thoughts and concerns, but also comes to stand outside the ordinary human community since "ordinary people think he is disturbed and rebuke him for this." The philosopher here does not accomplish a merely negative motion, standing outside the human. Instead, he accompanies this negative motion with a positive one, he "draws close to the divine" (249d). This "highest level of initiation" even amounts to "being possessed by god" (249d).

Nous and Hildebrandian Value-Response

We saw in chapter 2 that the turn toward the soul involves a turn away from the transient concerns of conventional life toward the sort of thing that would matter to an immortal, spiritual being: virtue and truth. We further saw in chapter 3 that the tripartite account of the interior structure of the soul motivated questions of self-mastery, identity, self-knowledge, and interiority. As we have proceeded further into this interior, we have discovered a more complex picture and have uncovered layer upon layer of intrapsychic contenders for the true person. First, we came to identify the person with the soul inside the soul–body composite. Second we came to identify the person with the rational aspect of the soul inside the larger tripartite soul. Third, we have now come to identify the person with the summit of that rational aspect: νοῦς. Just as we argued in chapter 2, this progressive movement toward a more and more spiritualized core may bring along with it the dangerous tendency to separate ourselves from and despise the lower, more material aspects of the total human person. Nevertheless, identifying the true person with νοῦς and further elevating this conception by describing νοῦς as the divine element within man is a profound movement toward personalism, laying a historical foundation without which the later developments and corrections would not have taken the shape they did.

Consider first the critical role that νοῦς plays in the historical development of "person" as a special category. What separates persons from non-persons? What makes "person" a different concept from "human being"? Historically, Gods and angels or other spiritual beings can be persons along with human beings, but not clams. Why? The central distinguishing feature is νοῦς. Gods, angels, and human beings have souls that participate in νοῦς—in some cases it may be correct to say that they simply *are* a νοῦς—while lower souls or inanimate material beings do not have this dimension to their being. In the contemporary literature on personhood and personal identity, many special features of persons are suggested, such as free-will, self-consciousness, memory, or moral agency, but all of these flow from the ancient conception of νοῦς. The story of just how these later concepts flow from the Platonic conception of νοῦς is a long one, but the common denominator is that all these capacities that we take to be especially characteristic of persons presuppose a grasp of intelligible forms "proceeding to bring many perceptions together into a reasoned unity" (*Phaedrus* 249c).

Consider also the way that "rational" or "intellectual" is used consistently as at least one of the differentiae in definitions of person throughout the tradition by such influential authors as Boethius or Aquinas. These authors of course mean "rational" not in the sense of discursive διάνοια but in the sense of non-discursive νοῦς, identifying the spiritual dimension of persons with the fundamental capacity to apprehend the eternal and intelligible.[16] Plato is not, of course, the first to use the word νοῦς.[17] Nor is he the first philosopher to make νοῦς a central concept in philosophy—we have already seen Socrates' complaint about Anaxagoras in the *Phaedo*. He is, however, the first author for whom we have any evidence that makes noetic beings a central category in his whole cosmological scheme and makes the presence of νοῦς in us central to the whole spiritual quest of the philosophical life. Hence, we are now in a position to identify at least one indispensable golden thread, among those we examined in chapter 1 that form the combined "rope" of personalism, as a "Platonic" thread—owing its origin and development to a deeply Platonic way of seeing the world that runs throughout Western philosophy—the golden thread of νοῦς.

---

16. In the passage right before his famous definition, for example, Boethius argues that the term *persona* is not applied to ensouled beings that lack "intellectus ac ratio," treating the two terms as synonymous, but to God, angels, and humans (*De Persona = Contra Eutychen* II). Notice that even at this early stage in the Latin tradition, Boethius makes this argument on the basis of the common usage of *persona* rather than a stipulated definition for theological purposes.

17. For an admirable survey of prior instances in Greek literature see T. B. L. Webster, "Some Psychological Terms in Greek Tragedy," *The Journal of Hellenic Studies* 77 (1957): 149–54.

Finally, consider the historical impact of identifying νοῦς with the divine. The language of divinity applied to νοῦς is more than mere poetic approbation. Our capacity to come into contact with the eternal principles of intelligibility in the cosmos is precisely what makes us "divine" because it involves a fundamental ontological kinship between the core of our being and the ground of meaning in the world. This kinship with divinity has a twofold impact on the way that we conceive of persons, both guaranteeing a fundamental dignity to all persons as persons and placing a transcendent call upon persons to develop further as persons. On the one hand, every single human being, just by being this kind of thing, participating in νοῦς, has a link to divinity.[18] As such, no matter how far we sink toward the life-world of plants and bugs, we still possess a fundamental contact with eternal intelligibility (*Phaedrus* 249b–c).[19] On the other hand, this link to the divine puts a hefty demand upon us. It is sufficient for cows to organically go on living the bovine life, but the unexamined life is not worth living *for a human being*—why?—because the very constitution of a "human soul" necessitates the presence of νοῦς and this demands that we undertake a quest of θέωσις. The divine above

---

18. This idea also arises, apart from the Platonic tradition, in Genesis 1:26 as the idea that man is made in the image and likeness of God. Very early in the interpretative history of this passage, however, the *imago Dei* is understood, rightly or wrongly, along strikingly Platonic lines. See for example Philo of Alexandria's interpretation in *On the Creation*, XXIII.69, where he identifies the image as νοῦς: "ἡ δὲ εἰκὼν λέγεκται κατὰ τὸν τῆς ψυχῆς ἡγεμόνα νοῦν." His following description of the ascent of νοῦς, driven by love, to a contact with and conformity to the forms, echoes closely the language, imagery, and structure of the *Phaedrus*.

19. Admittedly, it is striking how someone who holds this idea could fail to object in the strongest terms to such practices as slavery or infanticide. (The failure is even more striking in Aristotle, who actually undertakes a philosophical treatment of slavery in book 1 of his *Politics*.) We should "marvel at the immaturity in the understanding of the person that ancient peoples had who simply took slavery for granted; we think that it is as if they had hardly awakened to the personhood of human beings." Crosby, *The Selfhood of the Human Person*, 13. Compare the remarks of Burgos, *Personalist Anthropology*, 168. As Rist argues, it took even the Christians many centuries to fully wake up to the practical and political implications of holding that every human being is a person made in the image of God. He identifies the Spanish Dominicans Francesco de Vitoria and Bartholomé de las Casas as pivotal figures who finally begin arguing for the rights of Native Americans under Spanish rule on the basis of a principled application of this metaphysics, John Rist, *What Is a Person?* (Cambridge: Cambridge University Press, 2020), 82–83. Despite the earlier failure to apply the principle in a way that we would now demand, I nevertheless want to argue that this Platonic principle—that νοῦς is a divine element in all human beings—is one indispensable piece of the puzzle that combines historically with other key pieces, ultimately forming a total picture of universal personal dignity applying to all humans that, once pieced together, is hard to unsee.

man, that is, the forms, makes a perpetual call to the divine within man, that is, νοῦς. This call demands a response, first in the form of simply knowing and contemplating, but then also in the form of actively organizing our own lives and everything else within our sphere of responsibility in conformity with the intelligible principles that we have come to understand.

In this last section, I will describe a close parallel between the theory of νοῦς and *theosis* that we have already detailed and the philosophy of Dietrich von Hildebrand. We will use Hildebrand's philosophy on this theme as an exemplary representative of the personalist movement in general, since a very similar basic structure can be found in other personalists such as Max Scheler, Edith Stein, or Jacques Maritain, although these figures differ in the details. As we have seen, the Platonic spiritual quest involves (i) an identification with the highest, most divine element in us, that is, νοῦς, (ii) an active receptivity to that which νοῦς contemplates, that is, the forms, and (iii) the responsibility of the rational soul, participating in νοῦς, to organize itself and everything below it, as far as possible, in accordance with νοῦς. This closely resembles Hildebrand's account of what it means to be a person and the quest to develop as a person that this involves. For Hildebrand, we must (i) identify with our "free personal center" that we discussed in the last chapter, the divine and spiritual element within the human constitution, (ii) maintain an attitude of receptivity to objective, eternal, intelligible principles that he calls "values," and (iii) respond to those values by organizing our lives in accordance with them.

First, we should pause to expand our description of Hildebrand's values that we began in the last chapter to see how close they are to Platonic forms and how close Hildebrand's understanding of value-perception comes to νοῦς. Although this is not the place to give a full account of Hildebrand's general metaphysics and epistemology, we must first notice that values are a special case of what he calls "genuine essence," "genuine *eidos*," or "genuine form." These are the highest and most proper objects of knowledge and exhibit three characteristics: (i) they are necessary, (ii) they are "highly intelligible," and (iii) they can be known with "absolute certainty" through direct eidetic intuition.[20] Hildebrand credits Plato with achieving this insight:

> The great achievement of Plato in his *Meno* was the discovery that within the sphere of knowledge there are cases in which we grasp a necessary and highly intelligible state-of-affairs with absolute certainty. He saw how these cases differ profoundly from all other kinds of knowledge, and he appreciated the decisive importance of this distinction within the total sphere of knowledge.[21]

As examples of the kinds of essences that he has in mind, Hildebrand mentions such objects as triangles, being itself, justice, the color orange, the nature of will, or the nature of person. Within this broader category, however, a special class of essences are values, which are identified by the fact that they are apprehended as being intrinsically "important" in themselves and as calling upon us to make some adequate response. Values include moral values, which are predicable only of persons such as humility, forgiveness, purity, or courage, but they also include intellectual values, such as intelligence, or the value of an important discovery, and aesthetic values, such as the harmony between musical notes, the beauty of certain color combinations, or the resolution of a drama, along with several other kinds of value. While we encounter the manifestation of these values in particular instances, such as a particular performance of a symphony, what we apprehend when we apprehend a value is an intelligible essence that is timeless, necessarily related to other essences, and knowable with absolute certainty apart from the contingency of any particular empirical manifestation. We could apprehend with certainty the beauty manifest in a particular symphony even if we happened to be hallucinating the whole performance.

For Hildebrand it is essential to the personal mode of being that

---

20. The full treatment of this can be found in chapter 4, "The Object of Philosophical Knowledge," in Dietrich von Hildebrand, *What Is Philosophy?* (Steubenville, OH: Hildebrand Press, 2021). For a further discussion of the close link between Hildebrand's metaphysics and Plato's see Justin Keena, "Dietrich von Hildebrand's Critical Rehabilitation of Plato's Forms," *Quaestiones Disputatae* 10, no. 1 (2019): 110–23.

21. Hildebrand, *What Is Philosophy?* 59.

persons possess an ability to consciously apprehend genuine essences in general but especially values through an act of direct eidetic intuition. It would not stretch our terms in the slightest to translate this into Plato's language as νόησις. Hildebrand, however, makes explicit a point that, while not expressed in quite Hildebrand's terms, is congenial to much of the discussion throughout Plato's dialogues. Hildebrand argues that we must cultivate a basic "superactual" attitude of active receptivity toward essences (especially values) that he calls "reverence."[22] Insight into genuine essences may be possible without our looking for it—it may come to us as a sudden flash of insight, or it may be already tacitly embedded in our passive experience of the world—but our lives as conscious, intelligent beings will be deeply impoverished if we do not adopt a basic stance toward the objective world that is actively receptive to its intelligibility and, more importantly, to the call placed upon us by its values.

By "superactual," Hildebrand means that this stance toward intelligible reality is more than a mere faculty waiting to be actualized, and it is also more than an individual actualization of a faculty on one particular occasion. Rather, it is an active stance that we willingly and consciously adopt toward reality that then becomes part of the background condition of all our particular acts. By analogy, we might think of the attitude that a good husband adopts toward his wife. His love is more than a mere potency waiting to be actualized on particular occasions, and it is also more than a singular conscious act. Instead, his love becomes an active background condition of his whole life, fully sanctioned from his free personal center, but not necessarily in the center of conscious focus at some particular moment. While Plato would obviously not use quite the same categories as faculties and actualization, much less the notion of a superactual stance, I believe something like this idea lies behind the many exhortations to adopt the whole "life" (βίος) of philosophy, actively pursuing wisdom (for example, *Phaedo* 63e–64d9 or *Seventh Letter* 340b–341a).

As one adopts this stance of active receptivity to the objective world of meaning and intelligibility, especially the call of values, Hildebrand argues

---

22. See especially the chapter "Reverence" in Dietrich von Hildebrand and Alice von Hildebrand, *The Art of Living* (Steubenville, OH: Hildebrand Press, 2017).

that one begins to grow, not just intellectually, but as a person. One's internal world begins to expand and one becomes more and more sensitive to the hierarchy of claims made upon oneself by these external realities. In the very act of intellectually apprehending all genuine forms a person realizes the spiritual, personal dimension of his existence. In apprehending the importance of values in particular, however, and by internally responding to them in a manner that is "sanctioned" by the "free personal center" that we discussed in the last chapter, the person comes awake as a responsible person. We have already discussed Hildebrand's distinction between "person" and "personality," the former a basic endowment of the kind of thing that we all are, the latter a perfection that we achieve through our active participation. Here, however, I want to stress that it is a strikingly Platonic conception that Hildebrand has in mind, relying heavily on the role of *theosis*-through-νοῦς that we have detailed above:

> The more inner room a person reserves for the higher values, not letting himself be submerged by the less important ones, and the more he can actualize new dimensions in his soul when the higher values arise before his spiritual eye, so much more is he a genuine *personality*.[23]

Hildebrand even cites the passage of the *Phaedrus* that we discussed in detail above. He identifies the inner transformation of the person into a personality with the regrowth of the soul's wings as it begins to behold and feed upon the forms:

> And if Plato is right in saying that the soul grows wings as it beholds values, this act of beholding must be understood as an irradiation of the self by the Sun of Values, as a readiness to give oneself to, and to be immersed in, this radiation. The soul grows wings—that is, the deepest inner transformation takes place—only if there is a real penetration of values and a real self-forgetfulness is achieved.[24]

The deep irony here that Hildebrand notes is that the quest for self-knowledge with which Socrates began the whole Palinode leads to an

---

23. Hildebrand, *Liturgy and Personality*, 58.
24. Ibid., 4.

ecstatic, self-forgetful orientation toward the eternal principles of intelligibility.

We should not leave out, however, the specific element of *divinity* in this process. For Hildebrand, one's growth in consciousness happens in one way in the apprehension of all genuine essences, and there is some connection to the divine even here because such essences—as necessary, highly intelligible beings—must be rooted somehow in God.[25] Ultimately, however, we encounter the divine and become divine ourselves in an analogous and participatory sense as we apprehend and respond to values. Values do not present themselves to us, though, as homogeneous and equal; some take precedence over others. We must, therefore, ascend a hierarchy of values both in our apprehension and in our response. At one end, we may respond to quite common values in the little things we do every day, such as the beauty of the sky outside our window or the small kindnesses of common courtesy as we pass a stranger on the street. At the other end of the scale, however, we come to discover and to be transformed by the deep values that call for a profound, essentially religious, response to God Himself, the ground and center of all value.

Hildebrand argues that the Liturgy of the Church, especially that of the mass and the divine office, plays an indispensable role in bringing us into the space of the highest values before the face of God—hence the title of the book: *Liturgy and Personality*. Standing before the face of God is, for Hildebrand, the root "metaphysical situation of man":

> The only fruitful self-knowledge, and the only true one, is that which grows out of man's self-confrontation with God. We must first look at God and His immeasurable glory, and there put the question: "Who art Thou, and who am I?" We must speak with St. Augustine: "Could I but know Thee, I should know myself."[26]

---

25. Hildebrand, *What Is Philosophy?* 108. There is a difficulty here that Hildebrand flags because some essences, such as beauty or justice, are attributable to God in a way that others, such as the number three or the color red, are not. Although he declines to enter into the serious metaphysical and theological problems that this involves, Hildebrand hints that the latter must still be rooted in God in a manner different from the essences of contingent beings.

26. Hildebrand, *Transformation in Christ*, 47.

This "self-confrontation with God" leads to not only self-knowledge but also self-transformation. By orienting toward, apprehending, and finally responding to God, the "Sun of Values," the person is irradiated and transformed to be like God. Hence, *theosis* is the very process by which one is perfected as a person, transforming into a "personality." We might summarize this whole line of thinking by saying: *noesis* = *theosis* = personalization.

The I–Thou nature of this ultimate encounter with God should put us on alert. We have dwelt at length upon the parallels between the Platonic conception of *theosis*-through-*noesis* and that of Hildebrand, but we must now state several important caveats.

First, the objects of νοῦς in the dialogues, that is, the forms, are never spoken of as themselves persons. To be sure, *we* are characterized by personal language throughout the ascent, even at the highest point. Further, we are accompanied by a vast array of personal beings leading us in the ascent, such as the gods that lead the procession in the *Phaedrus* or the daimon Eros in the *Symposium*. Indeed, if one takes the mythic descriptions of the *Phaedo*, *Symposium*, *Republic*, *Phaedrus*, and *Timaeus* seriously, we inhabit a cosmos highly populated by noetic, personal beings who play an indispensable role in the life of philosophy. Even in the construction of the cosmos itself, we find the personal figure of the Demiurge, who is typically understood as a mythic representation of cosmic Νοῦς itself. Nevertheless, what all these personal beings lead us to is something else entirely, and our ascent takes us beyond the logical space of I–Thou interpersonal encounter to that of an I–It contemplation of impersonal intelligible principles. This extends to the ultimate ground of the forms themselves, that is, the good or the One.[27]

---

27. Notice that this need not be the case. Some later Platonic authors, such as Philo or Alcinous, come to conceive of the forms as ideas in the mind of God. On such a conception, the forms themselves are not independent persons but their ultimate ground is. Hence, the contemplation of any particular intelligible principle may be described in I–It terms, but the whole encounter must be embedded within a larger I–Thou framework. In even later Platonic authors such as Proclus, particular intelligible principles are even identified as personal gods. Much turns here on whether the Demiurge is understood as looking to a distinct reality more fundamental than himself when he looks to the model of the forms in the *Timaeus*. See T. M. Robinson, *Plato's Psychology*, 101–02, and Stephen Menn, *Plato on God as Nous* (South Bend, IN: St. Augustine's Press, 1995).

Hence, the charge brought against Plato by Gilson that we discussed in the first chapter is partly—but only partly—vindicated. On the one hand, Gilson was mistaken to identify "Socrates" in the dialogues as a merely accidental instantiation of the form "man." We have seen already, that Socrates is best identified first with an immortal soul, not analyzable in the same terms as sensible particulars, and second with the summit of the rational aspect of that soul, that is, νοῦς—even less analyzable in terms of sensible particulars. Gilson was also incorrect to describe in dismissive terms the concern that we find in the dialogues for the individual identity, responsibility, and development of "Socrates." On the other hand, however, Gilson was correct to identify the ultimate object of philosophical concern in the dialogues with forms that are described in impersonal terms. I have tried to show that this need not involve a loss of personhood on our side as we make our ascent, but there is a legitimate worry about the absence of personhood on the object side.

The impersonal characterization of the forms contributes to our second caveat: the fundamental role that *grace* plays in all Christian personalist authors. Because the forms are conceived in impersonal terms, there is no sense that they are coming to save us or personally bending down to draw us up the ladder of ascent. In some sense, the very nature of the good, and therefore all the other forms, involves a kind of "generosity," a free gift of intelligible being from participated principle to participant manifestations. Miller describes this impersonal generosity in the *Republic*'s famous image of the sun:

> The sun is a precise figure for that which, needing nothing other than itself to be itself, has, as it were, more than enough of itself. Nor does it hoard this surplus; rather, as if by a generous treasurer, this is "paid out" (ταμιευομένην) in a sort of "overflow" (ἐπίρρυτον) as the light which enables sight (508b) and nourishes all living things (509b). Thus, the sun is precisely not "detached" from what is other than it; on the contrary, *in being itself it gives of itself unstintingly*, dispensing the light by which everything else can grow and become. To extend this now to the Good: for it to be itself as "the perfect itself" is for it to be what it is as "fully" or perfectly as possible, and this is for it to suffice to itself in the form of

having more than enough of itself. From its very nature, therefore, the Good gives of itself. This essential "generosity" suffices for it to be cause of the forms (including itself) and of sensibles; it gives to the forms the perfection that each, to be itself, must have in the properly determinate way; and since each form thereby instantiates the Good, they too will be "generous," giving to sensibles the characters that these, to be themselves, must have in their properly determinate ways.[28]

Nevertheless, this kind of "generosity" needs quotation marks around it. It is not conceived as a personal gift from one *person* to another, the giver taking cognizance of the recipient and intending it for the recipient's good.

For our Christian authors, however, grace conceived as a *personal* gift forms an indispensable cornerstone of the whole philosophical and theological edifice. Our very existence is conceived as a personal gift from a personal God. Our whole ascent in the spiritual quest hangs on our receiving grace, personally given, from God. We stand in need of atonement, and that atonement is achieved not by the unconcerned, impersonal radiation of the good, but by a decisive personal act of God become man in Jesus Christ. To be sure, the dialogues give us ample material to think of man as "fallen" and in desperate need of salvation. It would be a mischaracterization to say that Plato thinks we must save ourselves and accomplish the ascent of *theosis* all under our own steam. We have already mentioned the indispensable role of the leading gods in the ascent passages of the *Phaedrus* and the *Symposium*. We can rightly describe their ministry to us as a salvific grace, and the manner in which we must humbly receive that grace is closer to the Christian picture than is commonly acknowledged. Nevertheless, these gods are mediators taking us up the ladder rather than the principle that they mediate at the top.

Within the later Platonic tradition this leads to a dispute about the centrality of theurgy to the philosophical life. Some, such as Iamblichus and Proclus, argue for its indispensability, while others such as Plotinus and Porphyry are more skeptical. For our Christian authors, however, the

---

28. Mitchell Miller, "Platonic Provocations: Reflections on the Good and the Soul in the *Republic*," in *Platonic Investigations*, 190.

dispute would not even arise as a question. The ascent of the soul must be accomplished for them in fundamentally religious and liturgical forms. Because it involves a personal encounter with a personal God, it must involve the categories of worship, prayer, thanksgiving, and communion, categories that can be applied literally, perhaps, to the leading gods, but only extended analogically to the forms or to the One.

This conceptual shift leads to an important practical shift. In several passages, we find the distinct impression that the salvation of the philosophical ascent is only available to an elite. While desirable for all noetic souls, the majority simply do not have what it takes to recover their prelapsarian contact with the forms, either because they do not follow in the train of Zeus or because they did not originally manage a full enough glimpse of the realities beyond the rim of heaven. This makes sense if salvation is principally a matter of philosophical contemplation—the many are manifestly not philosophers. If, however, we understand philosophical contemplation as a special case of the contact anyone can have with eternity through worship or prayer, then the ascent of *theosis* becomes possible for all by means of a grace personally and lovingly extended to each.

CHAPTER 5

Individuality and Uniqueness

As we saw in the first chapter, the principal charge against Plato by Gilson turned on the status of individual, unique persons in relation to forms. As we have seen, it is a mistake to interpret the individual person "Socrates" as just another sensible particular, but that has left us with some mystery about just exactly how we *are* to understand the individuation of persons.

In the material that we have already examined, Plato clearly speaks of a plurality of souls with individuating, qualitative differences. We may wonder, however, whether these individuating differences belong merely to an outer layer of the soul, external to the core of νοῦς. Perhaps we still have work to do, even in a disembodied state, striving for a greater and greater identification with our innermost self, as we argued in the last chapter, and we may worry that we are ultimately striving toward a core identity that is no longer differentiable between persons. Perhaps we are ultimately to merge into one Cosmic Mind or World Soul, something I will call the loss-of-identity thesis.

While such a direction of thought may suggest itself from a few premises that can be found in the dialogues, I will argue in this chapter that such a conclusion cannot be found in Plato and is ultimately antithetical to the whole purport of many of his best ethical arguments. If persons are not ultimately individuated from one another, then we lose the basic Socratic ideas of taking responsibility for our own actions and experiencing the consequences within our own soul. "It's better to suffer injustice than commit it," and similar Socratic maxims all rely upon individuated souls that each survive death and, even in the ideal state, remain one and the same, numerically distinct person.

This conclusion, however, may not deliver everything that a personalist might wish, and there are several lacunae left in Platonic metaphysics that will need to be filled in by later thinkers. Most importantly, one wonders about the *intelligibility* of the individual person *qua* individual. Naturally, the Platonic answer to the question, "What is it about something that we grasp when we find it intelligible?" is always going to be "form." But is there space in Plato's metaphysics for forms of individual persons? If not, can individual persons be known and loved *as individual persons*? Or can they only be detected, sidelong, so to speak, out of the corner of the mind's eye?

I will argue that forms of individual persons are compatible with a Platonic metaphysics but are nevertheless simply left undiscussed in the dialogues. Plato just did not get that far. There is an important methodological reason for this. Individual persons *qua* individuals are not the proper object of dialectic, and hence cannot feature in the passages of rigorous argument that are used to establish the forms. This is why so much of the material we have previously examined concerning the nature and fate of individual souls has taken place in passages of extended myth. Given his methodological commitments, Plato must come at individual persons through *mythos* rather than *logos*, but it would be a mistake to conclude from this that individuals have no place in his metaphysics or that Plato's heirs, such as Plotinus, could not develop from Plato's own premises a more detailed metaphysics of individuals. There's a lot of mythos in the dialogues, after all, and we cannot simply dismiss it all as mere fiction.

I will begin by laying out several important ideas and distinctions from personalist philosophy. While many of the terms introduced in this opening section are foreign to ancient thought and hence risk anachronistically reading ideas back into Plato, we must face that risk—cautiously and advisedly—because the questions we want to ask about the ontological and epistemic status of individual persons would be enormously more convoluted without clarifying our terms.

Personalist Commitments

At its heart, personalism involves an indispensable insight into the unrepeatable, unique dignity of each and every person. In order to clarify what this involves, it will prove helpful to draw a four-way distinction and (somewhat artificially) attach distinct labels to distinct ideas:

1. *Personhood*—Those ontological features in virtue of which someone is a someone rather than merely a something, for example, rationality or the capacity for moral agency.
2. *Personal Identity*—Those features of someone that distinguish him from all other persons as a unique someone in an incommunicable manner.
3. *Personality*—The full development of the features in both (1) and (2) into the maturity that we experience now to a degree but ultimately is only brought to full perfection in an ideal condition.
4. *Persona*—The conventional identity (often many identities) that we adopt as a kind of mask, present to others, and sometimes even come to believe ourselves.

In the above sense, personhood is common and shared, while personal identity is not. Both Peter and Paul are "individual substances of a rational nature," both possess free will or the dignity proper to personal moral agents or whatever else we want to say are the distinguishing features of persons as opposed to things. Such an ontological basis sets Peter and Paul apart from trees and rocks, but does not distinguish between Peter and Paul. Such features tell us *what* we are as persons, but they do not tell us *who* we are as *this* person. Granted, a particular instance of a general feature such as rationality is, as an instance, a particular instance metaphysically distinct from other instances. So Peter's rationality is metaphysically distinct from Paul's just as Peter's animality is metaphysically distinct from Paul's. Nevertheless, when we identify the unique and irreplaceable character of Peter's personal identity, we are identifying more than the metaphysical uniqueness that a particular pebble has—mysterious and wonderful as the pebble's particularity may be in its own right.

We have seen abundant evidence in the previous chapters that Plato clearly does distinguish between persons and things and his metaphysics gives us plenty of tools to account for this. Persons are a special class of souls, that is, noetic souls, possessing the capacity to understand "speech in terms of general forms, proceeding to bring many perceptions together into a reasoned unity" (*Phaedrus*, 249b–c). But does he likewise have the resources to account for personal identity, the distinction not between persons and things but between one noetic soul and another? That remains to be seen.

This distinction between personhood and personal identity may lead our minds toward those features of Peter that make him stand out from others in our experience: his brashness, his all-too-ready devotion to a messianic cause, or his bearded visage. But this would be a mistake. In the first place, such qualitative features are, in principle, sharable with others. As the scholastics say, they are *communicabilis*. (Note that "communicable" does not mean "able to be communicated in language"; it means "able to be *shared* metaphysically" since *communis* means "held in common.") While Peter's brashness makes him stand out from the crowd, other persons can be brash too. If the brashness were what made Peter Peter, then the others would be just as much Peter as he. Indeed, if they were *more* brash they would be more Peter than Peter. At *Theaetetus* 209c, Socrates suggests that Theaetetus might be identified, not just by his having a nose and eyes like all other humans but by having a snubbed nose.[1] Although this narrows the field down from all humans to just the

---

1. Note that in the context, Socrates is describing a view that he does not endorse for the sake of *reductio*. He is also describing not *personal* identity but, rather, the question of how it is that we come to identify any particular object at all.

handful who have a snubbed nose, it needs to be narrowed further until Theaetetus alone possesses the quality in question. The result would be "this snub-nosedness of yours [Theaetetus]" that leaves "imprinted and established in me [Socrates] a record that is different in some way from the other snub-nosednesses I have seen." The critical question here is whether or not such particular identifying qualities are shareable with others *even in principle* and whether they are qualities of the person *permanently and essentially*. For example, it may be the case that, at any moment, each person has a particular shape to his face that, if examined in close enough detail, would differentiate him from every other person on the planet, including an identical twin. Even if it happens to be the case that, on close enough inspection, a person's face is subtly a different shape from the billions of other faces, that shape is still the kind of thing that *in principle* could be duplicated. It is not *inconceivable* that there *could* be an exact duplicate of this particular facial shape. But it *is* inconceivable that there could ever be an exact duplicate of Peter—by definition, Peter is *this* person and no other.

Next, we might appeal to the idea that it is not just one identifying quality alone but the combination of several identifying qualities into a unique bundle.[2] Such a scheme, however, would face the same problems again. If the bundle of identifying characteristics is composed of nothing but shareable qualities, then there would be no reason to think that the bundle as a whole could not, in principle, be duplicated.

Understanding Peter's identity in terms of his striking features faces an even graver problem, however: Peter was not always brash, was not always bearded, and we do not know whether he will retain these qualities in the future. From the moment of his conception, Peter was Peter, an irreplaceable person, *this* person and no other. Hence, Peter's personal identity cannot depend on these acquired features. And while it may depend ontologically on those features we previously identified as essential to his personhood, it cannot be wholly constituted by them. His status as a noetic soul may be a *necessary* precondition for being who he is, but

---

2. This is the direction taken, for example, in Porphyry's *Isagoge*, 7.16–24. For discussion, see Sorabji, *Self*, 138–41.

Peter, Paul, and John all equally enjoy that status and so it cannot be the *sufficient* condition that we are looking for, the factor that accounts for Peter being Peter *as opposed to* Paul. Instead, we are left with a mysterious *remainder*, a dimension that goes beyond those features shared by Peter and Paul, yet prior to those features that Peter acquires in the course of his life. In the dark of those first hours as an embryo—or the first moments as a preincarnate soul floating off among the stars—Peter is already endowed with the dignity of personhood, but he is also endowed with the dignity of *being Peter*, a dignity that must be *incommunicable*, that is, "unshareable" with any other individual *in principle*.

When we pursue the inward, Socratic path of Delphic self-knowledge we find many reasons to think that our own unique personal identity is more than an unintelligible metaphysical surd. Nevertheless, we find an even better argument for the intelligibility of the individual person *qua* individual when we turn outward in love.[3] When a lover loves a beloved, his love is clearly motivated by something he grasps with his mind. He does not love for no reason, nor does he love a particular lump of unintelligible matter. How can we account for the intelligibility of the act of love and the intelligibility of love's intentional object? Again, one might be tempted to say that what the lover loves is the set of generic qualities of the beloved. Perhaps he is particularly funny, intelligent, and beautiful. But anyone who has ever loved will know that this falls short of the full explanation. The beloved's sense of humor or quick wit may be quite charming and they are indeed cherished, but they are cherished *because* they are the qualities of the beloved rather than the other way around. What is more, if the intentional object of love were some repeatable quality or even a complex bundle of such qualities, then love would love the kind of thing that could, in principle, be found to a greater degree in someone else—someone a bit funnier and a bit smarter—but

---

3. This argument is inspired by but not quite the same as that found in Dietrich von Hildebrand, *The Nature of Love*, trans. John F. Crosby and John Henry Crosby (South Bend, IN: St. Augustine's Press, 2009), chaps. 1 and 2. For further discussion of this argument and the necessity that the beloved qua unique, irreplaceable person be intelligible see John F. Crosby, "Personal Individuality: Dietrich von Hildebrand in Debate with Harry Frankfurt," in *Ethical Personalism*, ed. Cheikh Mbacke Gueye (Berlin: De Gruyter, 2011), 19–31.

this is the very opposite of love. If the beloved were replaceable, even in principle, by an upgraded version, then we would not have love but rather mere *use*. Hence, to the extent that the lover knows his beloved and is motivated to love by what he knows, there must be some metaphysical basis for this knowledge. There must be something graspable about the beloved that is in principle unique, unrepeatable, and attached to her as *this* beloved someone. Furthermore, love teaches us that this unrepeatable principle is not only intelligible it is also *valuable*, something that *motivates* the response of love.

This juncture is the point of greatest difficulty in reconciling personalism with Platonism. The foregoing argument has identified a dimension of Peter that is (i) intelligible and (ii) incommunicable. But it is difficult to have both at same time on standard Platonic assumptions. Typically, Platonists account for intelligibility by appealing to form. So if we can grasp *what it means for Peter to be Peter as distinct from Paul*, then there must be a "form of Peterness." But just as typically Platonists also account for forms by identifying a principle of intelligibility that can be instantiated in multiple particulars. The equal is just that principle by which every pair of equal things is equal, and the beautiful is just that principle by which every case of beauty is beautiful. A form is typically understood as a "one over many," in Aristotle's terms. If a "form of Peterness" works like this, however, then there could be, in principle, multiple Peters, and this is the very thing that we invoked the form of Peter to rule out in the first place. Is it possible, then, that one of these typical assumptions is mistaken? Either there would have to be principles of intelligibility other than forms or there would have to be forms of individuals that are incommunicable, that is, *not* a "one over many." Scour the dialogues as we might, all we turn up on either score is silence. Plato simply does not raise the issue we are pressing.

But this is not the end of the story. We can at least make space for these personalist commitments by ruling out several common misreadings of the dialogues and by showing that Plato is *not* silent on several other associated questions, such as the third of our key terms: *personality*. From the first moments of his life, Peter also receives a call. He does not remain an embryo or pristine preincarnate soul, and his destiny is more than the bare fact of his personhood or even the bare fact of his unique personal identity, wonderful as these may be. Hence, if I may be allowed to put it this way, we may distinguish between his "Peterness" as an *inherent* personal identity and his "Peterness" as an *achieved* personality. Notice that the former is not something that he could fail to receive or ever lose, but the latter is something to which he must live up through his free moral agency.

Hildebrand gives us a profound basis for these personalist ideas in the context of the Christian ideal of selflessness and the self-denial of the cross:

> Dying to oneself does not, however, mean the giving up of individuality. On the contrary, the more a man becomes "another Christ," the more he realizes the original unduplicable thought of God which He embodies.[4]

This "original unduplicable thought of God" that each and every person embodies establishes the metaphysical ground for both personal identity and personality. As Alexander Montes has beautifully elaborated, we learn from the Revelation of St. John that God calls each of us by a secret name written on a white stone.[5] Before Peter was ever even born, the unduplicable thought of Peter in the mind of God already differentiated Peter from Paul. While functioning as an origin point, this unduplicable thought of God also functions as a teleological endpoint, a calling toward which Peter is being drawn and an ideal to which he must live up.

In addition to these fundamentals, however, we also adopt various contingent *personae* that we present to others. Conventionally, when we ask, "Who is Peter?", common answers might be, "the manager who handles the east coast sales accounts," "that one guy—you remember—from college, who always made a fool of himself at the ΧΩ parties," or, more meaningfully, "my best friend from boarding school." These shifting "identities" run the gamut from more or less trivial functions within

---

4. Hildebrand, *Liturgy and Personality*, 19.
5. "Toward the Name of the Other," ed. D. T. Sheffler, *Quaestiones Disputatae* 10, no. 1 (2019).

a business to profoundly meaningful roles that we play in each other's lives. Nevertheless, personae are distinguished from the above three terms by being *contingent*. We can adopt and discard personae throughout our lives, sometimes quite easily, sometimes only with great difficulty, and hence they always remain external to our ultimate identity. This can be confusing, however, because a vast amount of talk today about one's "identity" is talk about personae. Teenagers, we say, struggle to carve out an "identity" for themselves, and by this we mean a way of dressing, talking, and walking that signals tribal membership to other youth. We speak of "identifying with" particular forms of music, political causes, or hobbies, and what we mean is that they provide us with a more or less coherent persona that we like and enjoy displaying to others. Further, the pull of such contingent persona can be so strong that the meaning of the other three terms can be almost entirely obscured as we come to develop our sense of self. A man may, for example, come to think of himself almost entirely as "an accountant at UBS," "Joanna's father," and "Larry's friend." Important as some of these personae may be, such a man may be in danger of losing touch with any deeper sense of who he is underneath the roles.

As we have already seen in previous chapters, Plato has much to say about this distinction between a fundamental *personality*, toward which we strive through ever deeper self-knowledge and ever-greater identification with our truest self, and the various *personae* that must be shed either in this life through philosophy or after death in the purgatorial wanderings of the soul. Many of the myths that we have already examined have this contrast as their focal theme, and it is precisely for this reason that Socrates again and again urges upon his interlocutors the Delphic injunction to know themselves. It will be helpful to keep this in mind during the sections below because I hope to discredit a common misreading of Plato according to which the shedding of our various personae are taken to mean the shedding of our personal identity as such, that is, the total loss of any numerically distinct differentiation between one noetic soul and another. Before we enter upon that argument, however, we must deal briefly with another source of confusion.

Individuation in General

As we turn to the Platonic material, we can begin by setting to one side a number of questions that, while very interesting in their own right and having some bearing on our central concerns, would take us far afield into difficulties that are the subject of an entirely different book. These questions include:

1. What individuates any one sensible particular from any other particular?
2. Are immaterial entities such as souls or minds individuated in the same way as sensible particulars? If not, how are they individuated?
3. Are forms individuals? If so, how are they individuated from each other?
4. What exactly is the relationship between individual instantiations of the same form?
5. What exactly is the relationship between an individual instantiation and the participated form?
6. What causes the instantiation of the same form into distinct participants?

Each of these questions can be approached both as questions about the actual truth of the matter and as questions about how best to interpret the text of the Platonic dialogues. All of them, however, must be carefully distinguished from the question that is the central focus of this chapter:

7. What individuates one *person* from another *person*?

Obviously, question (2) is closest to question (7) if we accept the identification of the individual person with an individual soul or mind, but even so, they are not quite the same question. When we ask *what* some entity is as distinct from another entity—even if the entities involved are human beings, souls, or minds—we are asking something quite different from the question: *Who* is this person as distinct from another person?

Several factors make the former questions easily confused with the latter. In English, especially when discussing the philosophy of personal identity, we commonly use the word "individual" with an exclusively personal scope, but we also frequently use it to refer to any particular entity. The situation is more complex with the derivatives of this word. Notice, for example, the distinctly personal ring in words like "individuality" or "individualism" that is less present in words like "individuation" (*pace* the common translation of Jung). It should be clear that there are a whole host of linguistic resonances in the first context that we should not import into the second, but it should also be clear that the reverse direction is not quite the same. The general metaphysical principles that differentiate one rock from another have *some* bearing on the question of what differentiates Socrates from Cebes. It would be a mistake, however, to think that once we have reached a conclusion about the metaphysics of rocks we have said all there is to say about the question of persons.

To further confuse matters, since ancient times, the general metaphysical problem of individuation has been discussed using named persons as stock examples. Most commonly, "Socrates" is the dummy particular (although the Stoics preferred "Theon" and "Dion"), through which we are meant to contemplate general metaphysical problems such as the distinction between Socrates and his snub nose or the role that his particular flesh and bones play in differentiating him as a distinct human animal from Cebes. In most cases, the identity of Socrates as a person is irrelevant. A particular tree or horse would have done just as well, and sometimes these are indeed used instead. The reason for using named persons, however, is easy to see. For most objects, we do not have a ready-to-hand linguistic marker for the particular *qua* particular. We can refer to *this* rock versus *that* rock, but when the whole discussion turns on distinguishing this rock from its being a rock, the necessary linguistic maneuvers become otiose. Much easier, then, to simply use an example that can be referred to with a proper *name* rather than a generic *noun*. We can then easily discuss the metaphysical problems involved in distinguishing Socrates from his humanity or Socrates from Cebes. We can and do, of course, name other things such as animals or places, but the examples that most easily suggest themselves are human persons.

We need to be careful, therefore, because there are some passages in the dialogues that may be tempting sources for us to examine the metaphysics of *personal* individuation when really they only provide evidence for individuation in general. For example, a famous passage in the *Phaedo* discusses the failure of particulars to fully explain their instantiation of forms. Socrates, Phaedo, and Simmias are used as the ready-to-hand examples and the question turns on the relationship between the three of them and the forms taller and shorter: "It is not, surely, the nature of Simmias to be taller than Socrates because he is Simmias but because of the tallness he happens to have" (102c). We may be tempted to mine such a passage for evidence of what Plato thinks about the personal identity of Simmias, but this would be misleading because the three men are being used here simply as examples of concrete sensible particulars with physical, spatial relations. Passages like this may have been what led Gilson to assume that "Socrates" is understood throughout the dialogues to refer to a sensible particular, merely an accidental, momentary participation in an eternal form, humanity. Just a few pages later, however, Socrates makes a point of saying that he is *not* primarily the sensible particular that could be shorter or taller than anything "by a head." *That* thing will soon be a corpse that Crito can bury anywhere he likes while Socrates himself goes off on the paths of the dead.

Merging with World Soul

Apart from personalist concerns, many interpreters of Plato have thought that the themes of the last chapter involve a total loss of individual personhood because they understand our coming to identify with νοῦς as an identification with some numerically singular impersonal reality.[6] A textbook example of this loss-of-identity thesis can be found in the classic and widely read introduction to Plato by G. M. A. Grube:

---

6. For different versions of this see, for example, Lee, "Reason and Rotation," 81, and Sorabji, *Self*, 34–35, 115.

As for immortality, the human soul as a whole definitely does not attain it, since part of it is unequivocally stated to be mortal: neither physical desire nor ambition survives. So that the human personality as we know it ceases to be at death. It is however said with equal clearness from the *Phaedo* to the *Timaeus* that the highest part of the soul, the mind or intellect, the capacity to apprehend universal truth, does survive. It lives on, presumably, as a focus of soul-force, that is, of the longing for perfection, beauty and truth, which is the ultimate origin of all ordered movement and life in the universe. If we ask further, how far this immortal mind keeps its individuality we must remember that from first to last the aim of the Platonic philosopher is to live on the universal plane, to *lose himself* more and more in the contemplation of truth, so that the perfect psyche would, it seems, lose itself completely in the universal mind, the world-psyche. Hence it remains individual only in so far as it is imperfect, and personal immortality is not something to aim at, but something to outgrow.[7]

For the personalist reading this exposition of Plato's thought, several alarm bells go off. First, when Grube mentions "the human personality as we know it," the qualification "as we know it" is doing a deceptively large share of the work. The same could be said for St. Paul (1 Corinthians 15:35–55), but no one thinks that Christian immortality involves a loss of personal identity. Certainly, the picture of our postmortem psychic existence that we discussed in chapter 2 involves the definite loss of many things we ordinarily take for granted in our embodied life as human beings. Does this license us, however, to speak of a loss of "personality" *simpliciter*? As our examination of the *Phaedo* makes clear, the whole thrust of the argument in that dialogue turns on whether *Socrates* survives not just some impersonal "focus of soul-force."

Second, we must also flag the equation between "the highest part of the soul" and "the mind or intellect." As we saw in the last chapter, the highest part of the soul, participating in νοῦς, is not just the same thing as νοῦς and remains definitely a soul. Grube also identifies "the universal

---

7. Grube, *Plato's Thought*, 148.

mind" and "the world-psyche," but this is to conflate the cosmic Νοῦς of the *Timaeus* with the World Soul that he makes.

Third and most importantly, Grube seems to waver here between two different senses of "individuality," when he asks how far the immortal mind "keeps its individuality." Is he speaking of qualitative individuality or numerical individuality? In the first sense, we may worry that ultimately, even if Socrates and Cebes do survive as distinct persons they nevertheless become more and more similar to each other, perhaps even becoming closer and closer to identical copies as they approach closer and closer to the ideal of perfect Νοῦς. In the second sense, however, we may worry that Socrates and Cebes ultimately merge with one another into a single νοῦς, perhaps a divine Cosmic Νοῦς. Grube's argument requires something like the following:

1. The only qualitative differences between two minds are those found in the contents of what those minds contemplate.
2. When perfect, each mind contemplates the same objects, that is, the forms or simply "universal truth."
3. Therefore, each perfect mind is qualitatively indistinguishable from every other perfect mind.

When he first speaks of losing oneself, Grube seems to have this picture in mind, as when we speak of being "lost" in thought. So far, we would simply have a plurality of noetic souls "lost" in the contemplation of the same object and thereby qualitatively indistinguishable from each other. When he comes back around, however, and says that the perfect psyche would "lose itself completely in the universal mind, the world-psyche," Grube seems to mean a more ontological sense of "lose itself," that is, that the object of our philosophical quest as noetic souls is ultimately to merge back with the World Soul, eliminating any numerical plurality. To go from the stated premise to this more profound conclusion, Grube would need to extend the above argument in something like the following way:

4. If two things become qualitatively indistinguishable, they must also become numerically identical.
5. Therefore, each perfect mind numerically merges with every other perfect mind.

There are problems with both stages of this argument. In the first stage, while we have some support for premise (2), we have no support for premise (1) in any passage of the dialogues. As we saw in the last chapter, the analogy of circular motion is meant to emphasize that the ideal activity of the noetic soul is always "about the same thing," the center point of the circle. But why should we infer from this that similarity of object and similarity of motion are all that differentiate one pristine noetic soul from another? Instead, we have more than a few hints that this is not the case. We find the division of different souls into the trains of eleven different gods in the *Phaedrus* (246e–247c) and the assignment of different souls to different stars in the *Timaeus* (41d–e), both of which refer to separated souls in a pristine state. Further, we have the idea that virtuous and vicious choices both contribute to building up a distinct character that persists between cycles of reincarnation. In the *Gorgias*, we find the "scars" that are superadded to the bare nature of the soul itself (524d), and in the *Republic*, we find the acquired τάξις of souls that changes on the basis of different choices (618b). Admittedly, the emphasis in both these passages rests on the ways that souls *degrade* by making vicious choices, but both passages include the possibility of making virtuous choices that build up a positive individuating character. In the second stage, we do not find premise (4) supported either. Something like Leibnitz's Law may be attractive to some philosophers, but we have no reason to read it back into Plato. On the contrary, we find Plato consistently and systematically distinguishing the same (τὸ αὐτόν) from the similar (τὸ ὅμοιον).

In place of Grube's picture, therefore, the following picture emerges as a plausible reading of the material: After death, our souls shed much of what we ordinarily take for granted in our embodied life, our sense-perception, our bodily hungers and pains, and all our reflexive habits of conventional embodied identity. The lower functions of our soul, the "mortal soul" that we read about in the *Timaeus*, end with our death, and this will lead, for many people, to a profound break with who they think they are. Nevertheless, that disembodied soul remains a distinct individual soul, differentiated both by innate factors according to its place in the cosmic scheme and by acquired factors according to its actions and experiences. In the cycle of reincarnation, souls can reach better and worse states, depending on both what they passively undergo and what they actively undertake. At the upper end of the scale, however, we find an ideal spiritual condition of perfect contemplation, and this state is the goal of the Platonic spiritual quest. As different souls approach that final ideal, they become, in one way, more and more similar to one another because they become more and more virtuous in the same virtues and because their activity is more and more occupied with a pure contemplation of the same objects: the forms. Nevertheless, this growing similarity need not involve any ontological merging with one another or with a Cosmic Mind. Distinct souls remain numerically distinct substances, with distinct centers of consciousness and distinct histories. Based on this picture, such ideal souls may even possess other qualitative differences that are not eliminated by the similarity of virtue and contemplation, such as the link to different stars or different gods. Different souls may just be innately different, qualitatively and numerically, even in the ideal state—Plato gives us no reason to rule out this possibility and several hints to rule it in.

The Mirror of God

After sketching this picture on the basis of evidence scattered throughout all the dialogues, we need to narrow our focus and devote extensive attention to one particular short passage in the *Alcibiades* because, more than anywhere else, this passage has been used to support the loss-of-identity thesis.[8] As we discussed in chapter 2, the authorship

---

8. Two well-known essays read the dialogue in this way: Julia Annas, "Self Knowledge in Early Plato," and David M. Johnson, "God as the True Self: Plato's Alcibiades i."

of the dialogue is controversial, so it may be unwise for advocates of this view to lean too heavily on it to establish Plato's own views, especially if the argument of the last section makes any sense. Nevertheless, I do think the *Alcibiades* is genuine because the principal arguments for rejecting its authenticity lean upon the ostensibly Neoplatonic character of the famous passage at the end of the dialogue—a character supposedly demonstrated by the loss-of-identity reading that we have already drawn into question. We need to face this passage head on for two reasons. First, I will argue that even if we grant the authenticity of the whole text, including the supposedly interpolated paragraph at 133c, we have no reason to accept the loss-of-identity thesis. It simply is not there in the text, regardless of which editorial emendations we accept. Second, we need to examine this text closely, apart from any scholarly controversy, for its intrinsic interest and the light it sheds on our central questions of personal identity.

Since the passage in question turns on the use θεός ("god") and the associated adjective θεῖος ("divine"), one word about terminology is in order. Throughout this section, I will speak of capital-G God not because I think the capital is required by the sense of θεός in this passage but because the view I wish to examine construes θεός here as a singular ultimate reality.[9] An easier, deflationary reading would understand our true self as simply *a* god among many, whose divine nature we can learn about by examining other divine beings like ourselves. Nevertheless, I want to consider what evidence for the loss-of-identity thesis really comes from this passage even if we construe θεός in as singular and ultimate a sense as possible.

The key passage begins at 133c, after Socrates has already argued for the identity of the person with the soul rather than the body or the body–soul composite (discussed at length in chapter 2):

> Then that region in [the soul, where knowledge and understanding take place] resembles God,[10] and someone who looked at that and grasped

---

9. Annas and Johnson construe the term in this way and capitalize "God" throughout their essays.

10. Reading θεῷ with Burnet rather than θείῳ. While I think the latter is more probable (in agreement with Johnson, "God as the True Self," 10 n. 23), the former lends the strongest support to

everything divine—God[11] and understanding—would have the best grasp of himself as well (τῷ θεῷ ἄρα τοῦτ' ἔοικεν αὐτῆς, καί τις εἰς τοῦτο βλέπων καὶ πᾶν τὸ θεῖον γνούς, θεόν τε καὶ φρόνησιν, οὕτω καὶ ἑαυτὸν ἂν γνοίη μάλιστα).[12]

In order to understand this provocative sentence, however, we must back up and understand the framing metaphor that Socrates uses to get us to this point.

Socrates begins, at 132d, by asking Alcibiades what we should do if the Delphic inscription had ordered our eyes to "see thyself," thinking that the eyes were men themselves. The trouble seems to be that the eye is the very thing by which an eye sees, and the gaze of that eye is always directed outward. We may think of the gaze as a ray that originates from the eye and proceeds in a straight line never to double back or bend upon itself. This metaphor tells us something important about the self and self-knowledge that may not have occurred to us without it. The self is fundamentally the subject of its own act of knowing and must direct that act toward an object, away from itself. If we are after self-knowledge, then, we must find some trick whereby the self that knows can also become the self that is known.

Alcibiades suggests an easy answer: Obviously, eyes can come to see themselves in mirrors. A reflective surface provides a place for the ray of sight proceeding out from the eye to bounce back and return home. The eye that sees becomes also the eye that is seen by existing, as it were, as a miniature copy on the surface of the mirror. But Socrates, even while agreeing to this, presses his own version of a mirror: "Isn't there something like that [that is, a mirror] in the eye, which we see with?" Socrates points out that if one person looks carefully into another's eye he will see his own face including his own eye. This is true especially of the very

---

the interpretation I wish to deny. The variation in meaning between the two is minimal, however, if we grant θεόν in the next line.

11. Reading θεόν with Burnet rather than the emendation θέαν, both because I think it is correct and because this reading would lend the strongest support to the interpretation I wish to deny. See ibid., 11 n. 25 for references to those who wish to emend to θέαν. Annas, "Self Knowledge in Early Plato," 131 n. 50: "[the emendation to θέαν] is both unwarranted and ludicrous."

12. Greek text is from *Platonis Opera*, ed. John Burnet (Oxford: Oxford University Press, 1973).

center of the eye, the pupil, where a miniature version of the man looking on can be seen.[13] But why should Socrates make this point rather than sticking with Alcibiades' suggestion about mirrors? If I have something in my eye, I do not rush to my wife and say, "Here, let me look into your eye so that I can see my own and get this out." A polished piece of metal or even the smooth surface of a pond would certainly be more effective if all I wanted were a reflection. Suppose, however, that I were a scientist that wanted to learn *what sort of thing* my own eye is. Under these conditions it would make sense for me to go to my wife and ask to examine her eye for the light it would shed on eyes in general and, by extension, my own eye. Socrates seems to have both modes of learning in view. Certainly he does make a point of the eye reflecting the eye of the beholder, but I suspect that he pushes Alcibiades to think about using other people's eyes because he also wants to incorporate the second mode of learning whereby we learn about ourselves by encountering and examining something of our own kind.

Furthermore, eyes have a structural feature, essential for Socrates' point, that mirrors and ponds do not. Eyes have an internal division between whites, irises, and pupils in a concentric arrangement. It is only in the center of the eye, Socrates insists, that the reflection we are after can be found. What is more, the central part of the eye is also the part of the eye where its most proper activity, sight, occurs. In this place, Socrates says that we find the ἀρετή of the eye. Because the eye in the metaphor stands for the soul, Socrates' move from flat and homogeneous mirrors to eyes is also a move toward thinking about the internal complexity of the soul. So far, the dialogue has treated the soul as a simple entity and the identification between the self and the soul has rested upon a negative answer to the question whether there is anything more authoritative about us than the soul (130d). Here, however, Socrates uses the structure of the eye to suggest concentric complexity within the soul itself and that the central region (τόπος) of the soul is the region where the ἀρετή

---

13. The word κόρη can mean both "pupil" and "puppet, doll" or "small votive image" (Liddell-Scott-Jones Greek-English Lexicon). See Johnson, "God as the True Self," 9, especially n. 17, for a discussion of the role that this miniature image played in ancient theories of vision.

of the soul, σοφία, accrues to it (133b). Although Socrates does not name this region, it seems clear enough that he is talking about νοῦς or τὸ λογιστικόν, where we are liable to find σοφία, τὸ εἰδέναι, and τὸ φρονεῖν (see below). By implication, this region of the soul may be more authoritative than the soul as a whole, calling into question the conclusion that the soul *simpliciter* is the self.

If we were to stop the chain of argument right here, we would have a clear lesson. Socrates would be saying to Alcibiades, in effect, "Alcibiades, if you want to know yourself you must look at the soul of another. Not just this, but you will need to look at the region of the other person's soul where the soul's proper excellence and activity are, that is, at the other person's νοῦς, if you want to truly understand yourself." But just at this point, Socrates introduces a whole new conceptual category into the discussion: divinity. He asks Alcibiades,

> Can we say that there is anything about the soul which is more divine (τῆς ψυχῆς θειότερον) than that where knowing and understanding take place (περὶ ὃ τὸ εἰδέναι τε καὶ φρονεῖν ἐστιν)? (133c)

Securing an agreement to this question allows Socrates to draw the provocative conclusion with which we began:

> Then that region in it resembles God, and someone who looked at that and grasped everything divine—God and understanding—would have the best grasp of himself as well. (133c)

Much of the interpretation of this passage hangs on how we understand the inference from Socrates' question to his conclusion. We might think that he reasons like this:

1. Nothing about the soul is more divine [in the strict sense] than the aspect that knows and understands.
2. This part is the self.
3. So the person who understands God and everything divine will have the best understanding of himself.[14]

---

14. This reconstruction seems to be exactly that of Johnson, "God as the True Self," 3: "[Soc-

Notice that (3) is just a repetition of Socrates' conclusion, and, although (2) has not been argued for, it seems to be where Socrates is leading us with the eye metaphor.[15] The crux of this reconstruction, then, hangs on reading "nothing more divine" in the strict sense.[16] Do we really need, however, the strict sense of "divine" to yield the conclusion that Socrates makes? Certainly if he had the strict sense in mind it would be big news, something that should be the conclusion of an argument rather than merely slipped in quietly. Instead, I suggest that he has something much weaker in mind:

1. Nothing about the soul is more divine [in the analogous sense] than the aspect that knows and understands.
2. This part is the self.
3. One can come to understand something best by understanding the model to which it is analogous.
4. So the person who understands God and everything divine will have the best understanding of himself.

On this interpretation, Socrates is silently drawing upon the notion of kinship between νοῦς in us and the divine. We continue learning about the self by looking at the soul of another, but we deepen what we learn by attending to that aspect of the other by which he knows and understands and the way that this aspect more than anything else about him mirrors the divine. Hence, we broaden our gaze to include both God and everything divine for the light all this can shed on our own nature.[17]

---

rates] suggests through the analogy with vision that one's truest self is the intellectual part of the soul, and that this intellect, being divine, is ultimately to be identified with God." This also seems implied by Annas, "Self Knowledge in Early Plato," 132: "[In this passage] knowing one's real self is knowing God."

15. Johnson, "God as the True Self," 8, attempts to reconstruct on Socrates' behalf an argument for this conclusion using the premises from 128a–130c.

16. See for example Annas, "Self Knowledge in Early Plato," 133: "Self-knowledge is not of the paradigmatically subjective, the embodied individual; it is of the paradigmatically objective, so that the true self turns out to be God, the ultimate reality."

17. The phrase "and someone who looked at that and grasped everything divine" is ambiguous between two readings. Socrates could have in mind two separate cognitive acts: (i) looking at the rational aspect of another person's soul *and as a separate act* (ii) grasping everything divine. Or Socrates could mean a single cognitive act, taking καί as epexegetic: looking at the rational aspect of another person's soul *and thereby* grasping everything divine. In neither case do we need to suppose

A few textual points support this interpretation. At 133b, using the eye metaphor, Socrates says that the soul, if it is going to know itself, should look at another soul, "and especially at that region in which what makes a soul good (ἡ ψυχῆς ἀρετή), wisdom, occurs, *and at anything else which is similar to it* (καὶ εἰς ἄλλο ᾧ τοῦτο τυγχάνει ὅμοιον ὄν)."[18] This addition expands the metaphor from eyes looking directly at the pupil of another eye to eyes looking at *anything else* that is similar to a pupil. Presumably this is based on the principle that looking at things similar to something will help someone understand the original. Further, in the primary sentence that we have been examining, Socrates does not limit the range of things that will help someone to understand himself to God but, rather, includes "everything divine" (πᾶν τὸ θεῖον), listing "God and understanding" (θεόν τε καὶ φρόνησιν) as examples. Surely the highest aspect of the soul is not to be identified in the strict sense with *everything* that qualifies as "divine." This advice makes sense, however, if the tacit principle is that if X belongs to class Y, or is at least akin to members of Y, then any member of Y will help us in some way to understand X.

So far, I have omitted any discussion of the disputed lines 133c8–17 because I think that a fairly clear picture of what Socrates means emerges without them.[19] When we consider these lines, however, we find further support for the idea that looking at God helps us to understand ourselves without implying that the self *just is* God:

> Just as mirrors are clearer, purer, and brighter than the reflecting surface of the eye, isn't God both purer and brighter than the best part of the

---

a strict identity between the rational aspect of another person's soul and everything divine. The second reading makes good sense on the principle that one can come to grasp something in the act of looking carefully at its analogue.

18. I agree with Johnson, "God as the True Self," 10, that the final phrase that I have emphasized must be retained as essential to the argument.

19. For a review of the relevant facts for and against inclusion of these lines see Johnson, "God as the True Self," 11–14, who favors their inclusion. See Annas, "Self Knowledge in Early Plato," 132 n. 51 for an argument against. Whether these lines are genuine or not does not greatly affect my argument. Annas thinks that the inclusion of these lines "spoils the metaphor" of looking into another's pupil, but only because she thinks the earlier passage means that "a soul should look at another soul, and *there* see God," that is, that God is "inside the soul." As I have tried to argue above, the earlier passage does not actually say this.

soul (καὶ ὁ θεὸς τοῦ ἐν τῇ ἡμετέρᾳ ψυχῇ βελτίστου καθαρώτερόν τε καὶ λαμπρότερον τυγχάνει ὄν)? ... So the way that we can best see and know ourselves is to use the finest mirror available and look at God and, on the human level, at the virtue of the soul (εἰς τὸν θεὸν ἄρα βλέποντες ἐκείνῳ καλλίστῳ ἐνόπτρῳ χρώμεθ᾽ ἂν καὶ τῶν ἀνθρωπίνων εἰς τὴν ψυχῆς ἀρετήν, καὶ οὕτως ὁρῷμεν καὶ γιγνώσκοιμεν ἡμᾶς αὐτούς).

If this text is genuine, Socrates returns to the option of looking to mirrors that he had earlier suppressed. Just as looking at a mirror will be a clearer, more effective way for an eye to see itself than looking at another eye, so too looking at God will be a clearer, more effective way for someone to come to understand himself than looking at the best part of another human soul. These lines give us a clear distinction between these two modes, one horizontal and the other vertical. The former may be useful but murky, while the latter is much more direct and clear. No one would think that looking at a mirror would help an eye see itself because the mirror *just is* the eye that is looking into it. At best, by applying Socrates' comments about the pupil, we find in the mirror a miniature copy, the reflection of that which is set before it. This would mean that somehow by standing before God and gazing into the divine nature one might find a copy of oneself in miniature. This would happen, however, not because the divine nature *just is* the self but because, like a mirror, it presents back a reflection of *whatever* one sets before it. At the risk of reading this passage anachronistically (after all, it may be a later addition), the underlying idea may be that, just as a mirror contains in potentiality the visible form of anything you can set before it, by analogy the divine nature formally contains all things *simpliciter*. As Hildebrand indicated above, each of us can find an "unduplicable thought" in the mind of God that establishes our identity before we are even born. At the risk of belaboring the point, however, saying that there are ideas for each of us existing in the mind of God is very different from saying that each of us just is the mind of God.

Be that as it may, this much is clear: God, along with "everything which is divine," is intrinsically more intelligible than anything in the human sphere. After all, while looking at the highest part of another human soul, one must sort through any layers of vice along with any lower aspects of human psychology that may get in the way. Looking straight at God (ὁ θεός), by contrast, provides a clear field for inquiry into what being divine (θεῖος) means. Ultimately this understanding will give us the best insight into our own true self because there is not "anything about the soul which is more divine."

The Self Itself

With this interpretation of 133c in hand, we are now in a position to tackle a puzzling passage earlier in the *Alcibiades* about which no one seems to agree but tantalizingly promises to be *the* key to our central question: Plato's understanding of the individual person.[20]

Socrates argues from 128a to 130c that the soul, rather than the body or the soul–body composite, is the self (ὁ ἄνθρωπος). At the end of this portion of argument, however, he qualifies their conclusion by commenting that what he and Alcibiades have agreed upon so far is proven "fairly well, although perhaps not rigorously" (μὴ ἀκριβῶς ἀλλὰ καὶ μετρίως). Instead, Socrates says they will have "a rigorous proof when we find out what we skipped over, because it would have taken quite a lot of study" (130c–d). This refers back to 129a–b, where Socrates alludes to another way of inquiring into "what we are":

> Tell me, how can we find out what "itself" is, in itself (τίν' ἂν τρόπον εὑρεθείη αὐτὸ ταὐτό)? Maybe this is the way to find out what we ourselves might be (τί ποτ' ἐσμὲν αὐτοί)—maybe it's the only possible way.

He expands on his requirements for the longer path that they are not taking:

> We should first consider what "itself" is, in itself (εἴη αὐτὸ τὸ αὐτό). But in fact, we've been considering what an individual self is, instead of what

---

20.. For several different interpretations of the passage see R. E. Allen, "Note on Alcibiades i, 129b 1"; Sorabji, *Self*; Annas, "Self Knowledge in Early Plato"; Johnson, "God as the True Self."

"itself" is (νῦν δὲ ἀντὶ τοῦ αὐτοῦ αὐτὸν ἕκαστον ἐσκέμμεθα ὅτι ἐστί).[21] Perhaps that was enough for us, for surely nothing about us has more authority (κυριώτερόν) than the soul, wouldn't you agree? (130d)

The cryptic and abbreviated nature of these comments makes it impossible to say anything conclusive about the nature of what Socrates means by αὐτὸ τὸ αὐτό.[22] Nevertheless, the reference to a thorough analysis of αὐτὸ τὸ αὐτό is too juicy to pass up without speculating about what it means, and reading αὐτὸ τὸ αὐτό as a singular ultimate reality identical to our true self underlies the arguments of Annas and Johnson when it comes to 133c. We must, therefore, consider a few possible readings.

The Neoplatonic commentators Olypiodorus and Proclus identify it as the rational soul (τὴν λογικὴν ψυχήν). I think that this identification is more probable than Johnson's identification of αὐτὸ τὸ αὐτό ultimately with God. As I read it, a clear implication of the mirror passage is that the rational part of the soul is a better candidate for the self than the soul *simpliciter*. A rigorous discussion of the rational part of the soul and its relationship to the divine, however, lies outside the scope of what Socrates hopes to achieve with the young Alcibiades here and now. On this reading, Socrates would be saying that he and Alcibiades know enough now to "pick out" each individual self (αὐτὸς ἕκαστος) from the vast field of other objects by distinguishing the soul from the body, but they have not properly understood the "*true* self" or "what exactly it means to be this 'self' that we have been talking about" (paraphrasing αὐτὸ τὸ αὐτό) because they have not undertaken an investigation into the nature of the soul and its internal complexity. In order to begin *that* discussion they would need to properly answer Socrates' question whether there is anything "about us" that has "more authority than the soul." While Alcibiades does not think that there is, Socrates is foreshadowing that "region" of the soul where wisdom, knowing, and understanding are (that is, νοῦς).

21. The manuscript text reads αὐτὸν ἕκαστον and this is the reading adopted by both Hutchinson and Johnson. Burnet emends to αὐτὸ ἕκαστον. See Allen, "Note on Alcibiades i, 129b 1," 188 n. 4, for support.
22. I agree with Allen, ibid., 187–88, that we can make some headway in ruling *out* some interpretations that are grammatically impossible. Primarily, I agree that the "itself" must be substantival rather than pronomial.

While I am sympathetic to this reading, there are two potential problems. First, the inclusion of ἕκαστος in the first phrase suggests that the more rigorous account will move away from a plurality of distinct individuals. For example, Sorabji understands αὐτὸ τὸ αὐτό as the rational part of the soul, but he also thinks that the contrast with αὐτὸς ἕκαστος precludes its numerical plurality in multiple individuals. He concludes, therefore, that we must identify the rational part of the soul and, by extension the self, with Universal Reason. Hence, the mind of Socrates (his true self) is numerically identical to the mind of Alcibiades.[23] Similarly, Annas argues that "my real self, if you like, is just the self-itself, and is not *my* self in any intuitive sense at all, since it is just as much your real self as mine."[24] She has further grounds for thinking this since she thinks that the identification of the self with the soul rather than the body means that the self must lose its individual personality. The implicit principle seems to be that souls cannot be individuated without bodies. Throughout, however, she does not make clear whether she means that there are a numerical plurality of selves that are qualitatively indistinguishable or simply a single self shared by all. This particular shift and the interpretation of it as a shift from plurality to singularity appears to be the crucial piece that Johnson needs for his argument that the self is ultimately God in the mirror passage.[25]

Second, the shift from the masculine in αὐτὸν ἕκαστον to the neuter in αὐτὸ τὸ αὐτό suggests a shift away from the personal into an impersonal register. This problem works in conjunction with the first because it reinforces the suspicions of those who want to ultimately identify the true self with a single impersonal reality.[26] Readers of other Platonic dialogues will also be familiar with the formula "the X itself" accompanied by a shift to the neuter as a verbal cue that Socrates means to designate a single intelligible principle (form) shared by multiple participants. Hence, Allen argues that αὐτὸ τὸ αὐτό should be understood as

---

23. Sorabji, *Self*, 116.
24. Annas, "Self Knowledge in Early Plato," 131.
25. Johnson, "God as the True Self," 16.
26. Annas, "Self Knowledge in Early Plato," 131; Johnson, "God as the True Self," 7.

the form of self.[27] On this reading, Socrates would be indicating that a full knowledge of each self cannot be obtained without a dialectical inquiry into the nature of what it means to be a self in general, the intelligible principle of selfhood as such. Along with Allen, I find this reading attractive, but we must notice that according to this interpretation we do not arrive at the conclusion that my true self and your true self are really identical to the form of self any more than one pair of equal sticks and another pair of equal stones are really identical to the equal itself. Instead, we would have the important but far less dramatic conclusion that just as understanding the equal itself is necessary for a fully accurate (ἀκριβῶς) understanding of the equal sticks and stones *qua* instances of equality, so too an understanding of the self itself would be necessary for Alcibiades to gain a fully accurate knowledge of himself *qua* instance of selfhood.

On any interpretation, Socrates is urging Alcibiades to reconsider his entirely conventional understanding of himself. So far, Socrates achieved a major victory with the handsome Athenian by getting him to consider the features of his body as external to his true self. The identification of the self with the soul as against the body, however, leaves untouched many other features of the personae that conventionally belong to one's identity. A rigorous and thoroughgoing move from the soul in general to the rational part of the soul would complete this process by stripping away even those more psychological features of individuals that serve to distinguish one from another. In the end, after removing Alcibiades' body and the peripheral aspects of Alcibiades' psychology, he will perhaps be left with a bare, naked mind, indistinguishable from every other mind. It does not follow from this, however, that we have arrived at Universal Reason, World Soul, or God. Interpretive moves which collapse the numerical plurality of distinct selves should not be taken lightly, and if Socrates had meant to say that my true self and your true self were really one and the same, with all the enormous ethical implications that would flow from this, he certainly could have been a lot more clear about it.

---

27. Allen, "Note on Alcibiades i, 129b 1," 189.

Conclusion

After the detailed examination of all these passages in the foregoing chapters, where have we arrived? Despite the sometimes bewildering variety of details in both myth and argument, we can form a remarkably coherent vision of the person—a vision that stands as *the* preeminent fountainhead of Western thinking about the person, the soul, and the self for thousands of years, without which the present development of personalism would be unthinkable.

According to the Platonic vision, we are, as persons, identical with souls, immortal centers of moral agency, responsible for our own actions and suffering the consequences of those actions within the very structure of the soul that we unendingly are. Currently, we are embodied and this embodiment carries with it both enormous dangers and enormous duties. Because of our embodiment, we are liable to be tempted into identities or psychological configurations that are lower than what we are really meant to be according to the highest aspect of our immortal soul. We are easily led astray by our desires for food, sex, and shoes as Socrates says in the *Phaedo*. We are also easily led into presenting ourselves according to the masks of various personae that prop up temporary but convenient ways of living based on our tribe, our career, our political position, or our rugged good looks. Despite all these temptations involved in our embodiment, we also have a duty to the body. It is the very nature of the soul to care for and govern the material world according to the divine order of the cosmos. If we accept this responsibility for the body and carry out our duties toward its governance well, we have the hope of improving our souls with virtue and carrying that improvement into the next cycle of reincarnation, ultimately proceeding on the spiritual quest of philosophy.

This quest is not limited to our struggles with embodiment because even apart from embodiment our souls have an internally complex structure. At one level, this complex structure is the familiar tripartite division into the truth-loving part, the honor-loving part, and the pleasure-loving part. At a more basic level, however, the real division is a bipartite division into the immortal and the mortal, that is, the necessary and essential aspects of our psychology versus the contingent and passing. By identifying more and more with the noetic pinnacle of our soul, we become more and more "lost" in the contemplation of eternal truth, conforming the "motions" of our soul more and more to the stable circular motions of the gods as they orbit the one center of meaning. Being "lost in thought," however, does not entail that we are ultimately "lost" like raindrops in the ocean. We never merge with the Great Noetic Soup. On the contrary, by more and more fully centering our contemplation on the eternal truth of the forms, we achieve more and more fully the mature personality that we were always meant to have. By doing so, we are participating in the very life of the gods and so become "divine" ourselves—but this should not be taken to mean that we "become God" in any ultimate, singular sense.

In each of the previous chapters, we have noticed several ways that personalists are rightly cautious about the dangers and implications of this vision. These worries, however, should not blind us to the ways that nearly all the key themes of personalism develop precisely from the Platonic tradition. While this often happens by way of development, disagreement, or correction of excesses, here more than anywhere else can we justify Alfred North Whitehead's famous remark that "the safest general characterization of the European philosophical tradition is that it consists in a series of footnotes to Plato."

Personalists have rightly warned against the danger that the dualism of the above picture poses because we are liable to alienate ourselves from our body (chapter 2). Instead, they emphasize the whole of the embodied human person. Nevertheless, the historical thread most responsible for safeguarding the dignity of the person as person against reductionistic or mechanistic thinking is precisely that Platonic strand that insists on the spiritual nature of the soul. Without this Platonic thread, personalists would not be in a position to worry about the alienation of the body—for the very notion of alienating the body from the self would be incoherent. Here, it is Plato who establishes the foundation because his account of the soul establishes an inner spiritual dimension of the person granting dignity, moral agency, and immortality. *This* dualism is the default position against which subsequent arguments are leveled in the West.

Likewise, personalists have rightly warned against the tendency in the Platonic tradition toward an overly intellectualized conception of the self (chapters 3 and 4). To some extent, this is based on a misunderstand of νοῦς, reading it as discursive, calculating reason rather than an affectively charged direct apprehension of truth. Nevertheless, the tripartite account that we sketched above does seem to leave out the will as a distinct faculty and the role of affectivity is left, at best, underanalyzed. Here again, however, this correction itself would be historically unthinkable apart from the Platonic groundwork. Plato sets the agenda here for the Aristotelians, the Stoics, and even negatively for the Epicureans. It is Platonic tripartition that is taken up by the early Christians, and it is the default beginning for all subsequent Western thinking about the inner workings of our soul and the spiritual quest to identify with our innermost self.

Finally, personalists have rightly wondered whether a Platonic epistemology can account for the intelligibility of the individual person *qua* individual (chapter 5). Are there forms of individual persons? While this remains unaddressed by Plato, it is not impossible to develop such an account on Platonic principles. Nevertheless, the question itself makes sense only within a tradition already saturated by Platonism, one assuming both the intrinsically valuable spiritual character of the person and the desirability of a metaphysically realist account of intelligibility.

Should we think of Plato, then, as a personalist before personalism? Hardly. Should we rather think of personalism as the natural and logical development of Platonism? Most definitely.

Index

affectivity, 14, 24, 90–91, 158
afterlife myths, 47
agency, 14, 56, 68, 72–73
Alcibiades, 20, 31–36, 52n36, 144–148, 152–155
alienation, 19, 22, 79, 157
allegory, 20, 82–83
analogy, 97–98, 100
anger, 68; anger, self-directed, 74
Aristophanes, 30
Aristotle, xix, 4, 6–7, 15, 43, 84, 91–92, 97, 117–118, 135
ascent and transcendence, 90, 114, 122, 127, 144
asceticism, 23–24; self-denial as Christian ideal, 136
Athenian Stranger, 28, 67, 98
Aquinas, St. Thomas xix, 2, 43, 117
Augustine, St., 2, 13, 86, 93, 123
αὐτὸ τὸ αὐτό, 153

beauty, 60, 85, 112; beauty, vision of (in Plato), 90

Boethius, 7, 117
body, xix, 14, 21, 32, 156; as clothing or decoration for the soul, 51; as image or semblance of the soul, 28–30; as impediment to knowledge and spirit, 37–38, 60; constraints on the soul, 41; devaluation and anti-body attitudes, 23–25; distinction from person/self, 34; instrumentalization of, 34, 58; ruled and used by the soul, 35

character and nature, 27, 53–55, 57, 157
Christianity, xviii, xx, 2, 16, 22, 158; conception of the person, 24; monasticism and Platonic psychology, 87; view of immortality, 20
christological councils, 5
Christology, 5–6
circular motion, 104–106, 108–109; as metaphor for reason, 104–106, 109; paradox of motion and rest, 106

159

cognition, 40, 105
communicability, 16, 132, 134–135
complexity and structure, 64, 83, 147, 156
conflict and harmony, 68, 72
conflict and motivation, 69, 72–74; appetite and desire, 72, 74; shame as motivation, 74
consciousness, xx, 7–8, 10–11, 13, 84; conscious subject, 39; consciousness and subjectivity, 39, 92; self-consciousness, 11; self-reflection, 10; unity of consciousness, 71
contemplation, philosophical, xxi, 127; contemplation, Platonic ideal of, 144
continental philosophy, xxi, 2, 119
cosmic order and judgment, 21, 51, 53–54, 56
creation, 102–103; responsibility removed from gods, 56; role of gods in, 103
Crito, 49

death, 37–38, 40–41, 48, 141; justification for hope in face of, 41; philosophical practice for, 37; pursuit of knowledge after, 41
Delphic injunction, xxiv, 4, 13, 32, 80–81; Delphic Oracle, 93
Demiurge, 101–104, 124
Descartes, René, 1
desire, 91
dharma (Vedic), 18
dignity, of the human person xx, xxii, xxv, 1, 17, 26, 118, 131 158
divine identity and naming, 53, 136, 146, 148
divinity, 98–99, 101–102, 107–111, 114–115, 118, 122–123, 148–150; as aspect of the soul, 59, 94, 97, 116, 152; deification, xxi–xxii, 17, 95, 97, 109, 111, 119, 123–127; derivative character of, 98; divine beings, 25, 50, 55, 60, 97, 101, 111, 124, 127; divine nature, 46, 97, 151; divine way of life, 83, 114; human participation in, 17, 101, 114–115; in relation to the soul and intellect, 110, 149–150; metaphor of rotation in Timaeus, 104; scala divinitatis, 101; the divine, xix, 17, 81, 96, 100, 112, 115, 145
Dominicans, Spanish, 118
dualism; anti-body, 37; dangers of, 157; radical, 23

early modern philosophy, xvii, xix, 1, 10
ecclesial communion theology, 8–9, 11–12
ecstasy (mania), Platonic, xix
education and development, 48, 112–113
embodiment, 42–43, 156–157; alien features afflicting the soul, 46; as essential to the person, 22; embodiment and incarnation, 9, 28; soul and body union, 43
Epictetus, 97
Epicureanism, xxiv, 20, 26, 93
essence, 5, 119–121; genuine essence/eidos/form, 119, 121; value as special class of, 120
existentialism, 1
external appearance; as disguise or decoration, 51

fate, 18; allotment of, 49, 56; and freedom, 15; inevitability in Greek thought, 56; necessity (Ananke), 88; Oedipus as illustration of, 56
forms, xxii, 43; concrete particulars as manifestations of, 96; general forms (εἶδος), 59; generosity of, 125; individuality of, 138; instantiation of, 138; intelligible forms, 117; of individuals, 135
freedom, xx, 65, 84, 88–89; emancipation from nature, 88; inner, xxv; inner personal, 89
friendship with oneself, 72

Gilson, Étienne 2–6, 8–12, 125, 129, 140
gift, 126
Glaucon, myth of, 81
Gnosticism, 23–25
God, 95–97, 123–124, 126–127, 136, 149–152, 154; image of, xx, 17, 97
gods, xxi, 101–102, 114–115; divinity of, 99, 115
Good, Form of the, 124–125
goodness, 112
Gorgias, 38, 50, 55, 57, 67, 143
grace, 125–126
Gregory of Nyssa, St., 93

heaven, 111, 127
Hellenistic Jewish philosophy, 72, 124; creation theology, 118
Heraclitus, 10, 28
Hildebrand, Dietrich von, xix, 89–90, 116, 119–123; emphasis on love, will, and affectivity, 90; ethics, 13, 15; Hildebrandian, 86; works, 13, 15, 17, 84, 89, 121, 123, 134, 136
homunculus problem, 69–71, 73
honor, 74
human being, 7, 23, 30, 44; soul-body compound, 21, 114, 116
hypostasis, 5

I-It relationship (Buber), 124
Iamblichus, xix, 31, 93, 126
identification, 80, 87; identification and personification, 70, 75, 79
identity, 51, 53–54, 57, 76, 144–145, 155; individuality, xix, 4, 7, 10, 128–129, 131, 133, 135, 139, 141–143; individuation, 129, 138–139
image, Platonic context, 29
immortality, 45–46, 101–103, 106–107, 141, 158; connection with divinity, 106; derivative vs. absolute, 46, 101–102; everlastingness vs. atemporality,
107; immortality of soul, 13, 30, 41, 48, 60, 111; impossibility for composite of soul and body, 58; in mortal beings, 103; personal, 45; and imperishability, 26, 58
incarnation, xviii, xx, 59
individualism, 139
intelligence, 40–41, 43, 104; See also Nous
intelligibility, 46, 119, 134–135, 158
interiority, xx, 13, 84, 91, 93–94; interior-oriented approach, 93; inward turn; Descartes, 1; inward-orientation, 94; path to self-knowledge, 26
interpersonal relations, 90
Isocrates, 27, 35

judgment, 48, 50–53, 55–56; nakedness in judgment, 50; requirement to judge by true self, 51; true self vs. external features, 51
just person, 79–80; image of, 79; rational part as representative, 80
justice, 77–78, 113, 120; as inner order, 72; as value itself, xix; desirability of, 77–78

Kant, Immanuel, 1, 17
Kinship Argument, 46
knowledge, 111, 113–114, 118–120, 148; absolute certainty, 120; as divine activity, 44; Platonic conception of, 100; participation in eternal intelligibility, 118; truth, 2, 116, 142

language and communication, 39, 49
laws, 20; capacity of sanctioning, 85
Laws (Plato), 28, 67, 69, 98, 105
legal personhood; Roman law, 16
Leontius, 73–76, 80
life (βίος), 21, 57, 59, 121
liturgy, 123
logos, 66, 87, 103
love, 134–135

INDEX

Maritain, Jacques 2, 119
Maximus the Confessor, St., 93
medieval mystical tradition, 1, 87
medieval philosophy, 3–5, 16
memory and recollection, 42–45, 59; episodic memory, 45
Meno, 28, 31n17, 42, 120
metaphysics, 85, 139; imitation, 109; participation, 3, 127
mirror metaphor, 150–151; in relation to self-knowledge, 146
modern philosophy, 1–2, 119
moral agency, 10–13, 84, 158; moral responsibility, 12–13, 18, 55
mortality, 46, 101
mystery religions; Orphic tradition, 12, 27; Pythagorean tradition, 10, 12, 27
mythological imagery; chariot image, 110; composite nature (Chimera, Cerberus), 77; contrasted with true account, 50

nous, 14, 27, 66, 95, 100, 103, 106–109, 111–112, 116–117, 119, 125, 127, 148; as cognitive act, 107; as model of mind, 106; as steersman, 83; as virtue, 107; cosmic mind, 18, 124, 129, 142, 144; divine activity and order, 108; intellect, xxi, 8, 117, 149; noesis, 121, 124; *See also* Intelligence

One, the (Neoplatonic), 124, 127
origin and wandering, 103, 137
ownership and distinction, 33

Parmenides, 38, 97
Paul, St., 141
perception, 39, 60
Peripatetics, 20, 93
person, xx, xxiv–xxv, 2–4, 7, 10–13, 21–22, 24, 28–29, 34–36, 42, 51, 72, 78–79, 83–89, 119–120, 152; as rational, moral, free, self-determining, responsible, 10; capacity for volitional freedom, 86; concept of, 5, 11, 21, 116; core of the person, 16; distinction from body, 34; forms of individual persons, 130; free personal center, 87–88, 119; identification with the soul, 21, 32, 35; individual soul vs. individual human being, 46; inner person, 78; intrinsic worth, xxv, 26; metaphysics of, 130, 132; moral agency, xxiv; person, Platonic vision of, 156; personal being in cosmology, 124; personal identity, 15, 44–45, 54, 60, 65, 131–134, 136, 139–140, 143, 145; personality, 9–10, 44, 54, 57, 89–91, 122–123, 131, 135–137; personalization, 124; personhood, 8, 31, 41, 55, 117–118, 125, 131–134, 140; selfhood, 17, 85, 118, 134, 137, 155; spiritual character of, xxiv, 158; vision of, 156

persona, 5, 131, 136–137
personalism, xviii–xxi, xxiii–xxvii, 1–3, 6–7, 11–14, 16–20, 22–27, 64–65, 86, 89, 116, 119–120, 130–131, 135, 158; charges against Plato, 1, 3; Christian, xix, xxiii, xxv, xxvii, 6, 16, 24, 26, 62, 120, 126, 138, 144; Christian personalism, xxiv; contemporary, xxv; contrast with cosmological conception, 91; core ideas, 84; core themes, 65; critique of body-self analogy, 34; development of, 27, 156; lacunae in Platonic metaphysics, 130; objections to dualism, 23, 25; personalist anthropology, 14, 118; personalist movement, 119; personalist philosophy, xxv, 13, 16, 24; personalist reading of Plato, 20; personalist understanding of the human being, 7; proto-personalist concerns in Plato, 94; roots in

INDEX

conversation, 36; twentieth-century, xxiv; uniqueness and incommunicability of the person, xx; view of the self, 14
Phaedo, 19–20, 23, 30, 37, 40, 45, 47–49, 52, 55, 58–59, 63–64, 69, 88, 106, 117, 124, 140–141
Phaedrus, 20–21, 36, 44, 48, 58–59, 80, 90, 99–100, 107, 110–115, 117–118, 122, 124, 126, 132, 143
Philebus, 20, 97
Philo of Alexandria, 72, 118, 124
Philokalia, 87
philosophers, ancient, 38, 93, 99, 115
philosophical anthropology, 35, 66, 118, 130; Christian anthropology, xxv, 6; theological anthropology, xxii, 2, 4–7, 11–13, 16, 84, 86, 91, 93, 123; *See also Aristotelian Anthropology*
philosophical life, xxi–xxii, 49, 82, 115, 117, 156
Pindar, 28
Plato; ancient influences on Plato, 40; ascent, Platonic, 91; authenticity of dialogues, 145; cosmic nous in Plato, 100; cosmology, xxiv; epistemology, 90, 158; essence and existence distinction, 6; forms, xviii, xxiv, *see also* forms; 85; metaphysics of, xxiii, 4, 6, 19, 25, 27, 63–64, 87, 96, 113, 158; on the Good, 126; on the self, 152; pederastic conception of love, 90; philosophical quest priority, 92; Platonic scholarship, 20, 37, 69, 71, 78; Platonic school, xxiv; rational part as true self, 78; rebirth in myths of, 48; reincarnation cycle of, 144; self-control, xx; theory of mind, 39; Third Man Argument, 97; world of true reality, xxii; ἔρως (Eros) as central theme, 90; *see also* Forms
Platonic tradition, 3, 26, 117, 157; Christian-Platonic relations, xvii, xix, xxv, 2; gods in Platonic ascent, 124; Neoplatonism, xix, 86, 126, 145, 153; Platonism, xix, xxiii, xxv, 2, 9, 19, 25, 93, 119, 135, 158; Plotinus and Enneads, 1, 10, 91, 93, 126, 130; post-Platonic philosophy, 158; Timaeus hierarchy of divinity, 101; Timaeus on reason as order and proportion, 104
Plotinus, 1, 10, 91, 93, 126, 130
pre-Socratic philosophy, 10, 28, 38, 88, 117
Proclus, xix, 31, 93, 124, 126, 153
psychological principles, 71, 75
Pythagoreanism, 10, 12, 27, 40

rational faculties, 13, 73, 76; belief and cognition in non-rational parts, 71
rationality, 66, 117
Ratzinger, Joseph 4–6, 11–12, 16
reason, 39, 59, 74, 87, 96, 104, 108, 117, 154
receptivity, 113, 121
religious and philosophical synthesis, xxii, 24, 100
religious traditions, 23; funeral customs, 49; reincarnation doctrine, 9, 143, 156
Republic, 29, 48, 63–64, 66, 69–70, 72, 75–77, 82, 87, 103, 124–125, 143; 588b–e, 77; 589a–b, 79; image of the sun, 125; metaphor of the city and the soul, 70; Myth of Er, 15, 18, 55–56, 88; story of Leontius, 74
resurrection, xviii
Richard of St. Victor, 5, 16
rights, communicable and incommunicable, 16

sacraments, xviii, 127
salvation, 126–127; atonement and forgiveness, 85, 126; grace and predestination, 18, 127
Scheler, Max 119
Second Apology (Socrates's), 40–41
self, 1, 8, 14, 26, 31, 33, 64, 69, 71–74, 87, 148, 153–155

self-control, 65–68, 113; general concept, 66, 88, 111; mastery of oneself, 67; self-mastery, 65, 68, 84
self-cultivation, 32–33; requires self-knowledge, 32
self-effacement, 109; passivity, 14; self-forgetfulness, 122
self-knowledge, xx, 13, 81, 93, 99, 123, 137, 146–147, 149–152; as path to personal identity, 65; through encounter with others, 147; vertical vs. horizontal modes, 151
sexuality, 24
slavery, violation of dignity, 17
Socrates, xvii–xviii, xxi, 3, 10, 13–16, 18, 20–22, 29, 32–38, 40–50, 52, 54, 56–58, 60–61, 63–64, 66–68, 71–74, 76–79, 81–83, 93, 99, 107, 110, 112, 114–115, 117, 122, 125, 129–130, 132–134, 137, 139–142, 146–156; paradoxes and maxims, 26, 130
Soul; appetitive part, 73; as identified with the person, 4; body-soul relationship, xxiii, 23–24, 29, 32, 35, 37, 39, 46, 49, 58, 65, 155; choice (αἵρεσις) of, 21; cosmological conception of the soul, 92; identification with the person, xx; identity with self, 50; noetic beings and souls, 88, 117, 132–133, 141, 143; noetic soul, 14; parts and divisions, 63, 66–67, 69, 71, 73, 75–76; rational aspects, 64, 95, 103, 116, 149, 153, 155; rational part (of the soul), 79–80, 96; rational part (νοῦς), 65; rational part and its relation to Universal Reason, 108; rational part as human, 77; soul, continuity of consciousness, 41, 47; soul, disembodied existence, 38, 43, 45; soul, immortality of, 21, 24, 27, 40, 42, 47, 110, 156; soul, individuation and identity, 9, 52, 129–130, 138, 144, 154; soul, mortality of, 144; soul, pre-existence, 42–44; soul, survival and fate after death, 40–41, 48, 52; soul, tripartite theory, 61, 63–67, 69–71, 73, 75, 77, 81–84, 86, 88, 90, 92–94, 116, 158; world soul, 41, 97, 109, 129, 141–142
spiritual emancipation, 15, 88
spiritual reality, xvii, 96, 107, 110, 112, 117, 120–121
Stein, Edith 119
Stoicism/Stoics, 1 6, 10–11, 15, 20, 86, 93, 97, 139;
Stranger, 29, 105–106
Symposium, 20, 30, 90, 124, 126
subjectivity, 7, 109

Theaetetus, 95, 97, 132–133
Timaeus, 9, 20, 88, 97, 100–103, 105–106, 108, 124, 143
transcendence, xx
transformation; ideal self, 76; inner transformation through beholding values, 122
truth, 39, 55, 66, 113, 116, 141–142, 157–158
two-worlds doctrine, 95
tyranny, 57

union with the divine, 94
uniqueness, 128–129, 131, 133, 135, 143; and unrepeatability, 9; of individual person, xxii; of individuals, 15
Universal Reason, 96, 108, 154–155
universals and particulars, xxiii

values, xix, 119–123; aesthetic value, 120; as genuine essence/eidos/form, 119; as intrinsically important and calling for response, 120; call of, 121; hierarchy of, 122–123; intellectual value, 120; objective value, 15,

84–85; value-perception, 119; value-response, 85, 116, 122
virtue, 26, 53, 56–57, 116, 143; courage, 70; measure, proportion, and orderliness as features of, 107; moderation, 68, 70; of the eye (aretē), 147
vision and perception, 69

will, 84, 86, 89–90, 120–121, 131, 158; free will, 11, 13, 18, 55

wisdom (phronesis), 41, 43, 112, 121, 148, 150
Wojtyła, Karol 6–7, 11–12, 84, 91–92
World Soul, 18, 41, 97, 100, 109, 124, 129, 140–142, 144, 155
Worship, prayer and reverence, 121, 127; thanksgiving, 127
worth, infinite worth and dignity of the person, 89; *see also* Dignity
Zeus, 50–51, 55, 60, 97, 102, 111, 127

www.ingramcontent.com/pod-product-compliance
Lightning Source LLC
Chambersburg PA
CBHW071742150426
43191CB00010B/1660